With FRIENDS Like These, Who Needs Enemies?

Kennedee Devoe

PUBLICATIONS

Written and created by: Kennedee Devoe

Editor: Jill Duska

Cover Design: Donna Osborne Clark

Interior Design: Devoe Publications

Typesetting: The Book Biz

Back Photo: Khristal King

ISBN-13: 978-0989987127

ISBN-10: 0989987124

Published by: Devoe Publications

Dedication

To my real ride or dies...I appreciate all of you and love to you to pieces.

Acknowledgments

First and foremost I would like to thank God, from whom all my blessings come from. Without you, I am nothing. To my mama, Ms. King, thank you for encouraging me to continue to pursue my dreams. I love you so much, and I appreciate everything you and Dad were to me while growing up. To all my family who have supported this endeavor, I truly appreciate you. Special thanks to Kelley. A very special thank you to Frances Ricks for reminding me that if I dug deep down inside, I'd find something else to write about. Debbie, Hermina, Martha, Jill, and Revel, thank you for allowing me to get on your nerves. I appreciate you and all your feedback. To all my friends, associates, and acquaintances, thank you so much for supporting me and for the word of mouth about the book. To my former companion of 5 ½ years, I thank you for your contributions behind the scenes with the first book to assist in its success. It's just too bad you didn't read the book to learn better to do better than those before you. I wish you well. To Mr. Jason Frost at Russo's Books, words cannot express the gratitude that I have for you. Thank you so much for being the first bookstore to carry my book. This literary industry is no joke. Thank you so much Benny Bennassi, Blacc Top, Michael McGrew, and Hasani Pettiford for your guidance. Special thanks to Lisa Borders Muhammad for holding my hand through this process. Thank you to all the Facebook reading groups, blog talk radio shows, book promoters, and book clubs for the love and support. This journey couldn't be possible without my reader friends and family that I've made along the way. While it is impossible to thank each of you, all I can say is thank you, thank you, thank you from the bottom of my heart for giving me a chance as a new author, and for making *Two Wrongs Don't Make a Right...It Makes Us* Even an Amazon Bestseller. I appreciate you all so much. I'm sure I probably forgot someone, but it wasn't with intent, so please charge it to my head and not my heart.

"Wishing to be friends is quick work, but

friendship is slow-ripening fruit."

-Aristotle-

Let the Show Begin

In this decade, we've been plagued with reality shows like _Love and Hip Hop, Basketball Wives_, and my favorite, _Real Housewives of Atlanta._ These shows have gained a bad rep for glamorizing drama, fighting, and supposedly showcasing African American women in a negative way. But truth be told, if you turn to any reality show there is bound to be some drama in spite of the race of the cast, hence _Mob Movies, Real Housewives of New Jersey or Real Housewives of New York_, etc., etc. Let's be honest: some of our friendships in real life would make a good episode on all of these reality shows. Don't pretend like you've never gotten mad at a friend, had a small falling out, agreed to disagree to keep the peace, or even felt like slapping the ish out of your friend. If you are sitting there saying, "Nah, my friendships are perfect", well kudos to you, honey, because some people have never experienced a friendship that is perfect.

Hi, my name is Kennedee. My friends and family call me KD. However, you may know me as Kennedee Devoe, author of *Two Wrongs Don't Make a Right...It Makes Us Even*. I was so elated that my supporters enjoyed reading my first book. I have definitely been through some crazy things in my life, and I was happy that the story was received so well amongst readers. I was torn for a while if I wanted to write another book because my supporters wanted a sequel to the first book.

However, I thought I'd go in a different direction with my second book. While cleaning up today, I came across some old photo scrapbooks, and started flipping through the pages. A smile came across my face as I looked at the wonderful memories that I had made back in junior high school with a crew of girls I ran with. We did everything together, and as I thumbed through the pages, I saw so many written captions that said "Friends Forever". That's when it hit me that I'd write a book about my friendships with a group of girls that I had known since I was thirteen years old. I thought about it for a bit and thought it was a bad idea because I didn't want to be associated with drama. Then I thought about how I like being an open book by allowing others to take a walk down memory lane through my stories and say,

"Hey, that happened to me too" or for someone to see into my life to learn, grow, and build from all of my life experiences.

So I decided to roll with this story because I am comfortable with who I am and what I have been through in my life. I've learned my best lessons in the worst ways. I have only used my experiences with everything that has happened to help me become stronger, wiser, and better. I found all my old scrapbooks that I had put away, pulled them out, and turned each of them page by page. I looked at the pictures and I thought back on the fun and crazy times I shared with these ladies from my teens to my mid-30's. I came across a page where I had written "Friends Forever". A tear came to my eye as I took my index finger and rubbed it over the words while thinking to myself, *Well, honey, forever must have meant ten years, twelve years, twenty years, etc., but we sho' couldn't make it last forever like Keith Sweat said.*

Although there are no exact rules or guidelines when it comes to any friendship or measurement of loyalty, there are some rules to this shit, just certain things that just shouldn't have to be said. In case you're oblivious, let me help you understand. In a friendship, there has to be some type of loyalty. Otherwise, it's just not going to work. You can't be bad-mouthing a friend because that's just bad business. If I'm not around, and you just sit by and LET my enemy talk greasy 'bout me in front of you...then you become the enemy too. The truth hurts, but it shall set you free, and I'd rather a real friend tell me the truth than hurt me with a lie. The

MOST sacred rule of all is don't be sleeping or

talking to your friends' exes. That right there alone

will get you cut or cut out of the friendship.

Loyalty, respect, integrity...in that order. There was

one rule that just had to be said: don't casually use

the word "bitch" with me. Calling each other

"bitch" was not a term of endearment for me. Using

that word meant that shit just got real with us and

it had just turned into an earring removal moment,

the opening of a can of whip ass.

I guess the rules must have changed as we got older.

These are the women I considered my best friends,

but that didn't mean I knew them well. My motto

was if you rock wit' me, I rock wit' ya. Couldn't

nobody mess that up, but you. However, these

ladies would soon test my logic as well as my loyalty, character, and integrity and show me the true meaning of friendship.

2

Allow Me to Introduce Us

I can remember it like it was yesterday. In 1988, my parents had just enrolled me in a private Christian school a few miles from the house. It was a small, quaint school with no more than 300 students. I was in junior high school, where I would meet four young ladies who would show me the true meaning of what friendship was or wasn't. They say friendship is born at that moment when one person says to another, "What! You too? I thought I was the only one!" Well, that's exactly how it happened. I don't want to get into a long, drawn-out story about the golden days, because to me it seems irrelevant. This story ain't about no Kumbaya moments in the friendship.

Allow me to introduce you to the crew, but before I get started, let me just say that of course I've changed their real names. The crew consisted of Emil, Chloe, Sage, and Talia. Emil was short, about 5'2". She was mixed with Indian and Black. No, for real, she really had Indian in her family. Her mom was Blackfoot Indian and her dad was Black. She had the prettiest honey-brown complexion I'd ever seen. Her hair was thick, long, and jet black. She was very pretty, but self-centered. She was so conceited sometimes that she often viewed us as her competition rather than her friends. She was really nonchalant and quite dismissive about the opinion of others. And boy, oh boy could she flirt!

Sometimes she could be a downright airhead about her ways.

Chloe was tall like me, a very thin white girl with light freckles and sandy brown hair. Her teeth were a li'l jacked up, and she was in dire need of braces. She wasn't shy at all. She was very outspoken, a li'l too much for my taste. I think to describe her best would be in the words of Jay-Z: as loud as a motorbike, but wouldn't bust a grape in a fruit fight. She was just all talk. She was definitely the hothead of the group.

Sage was about 5'3", Puerto Rican with blondish-red curly hair and a sassy around-the-way-girl feel to her and a whole lot of confidence. She was a li'l on the thick side to be a junior high schooler, and she liked to talk a lot, meaning telling everyone's business. It was okay then because she usually just told our business within the circle. That just meant that sometimes everyone found out some things before they needed to know. But you still had to be careful with her and tell her that what you were telling her was private and for no one else to know. Even if you'd tell her that, you'd still have to wonder if she was capable of keeping that mouth shut.

Talia was 5'4" tall, skinny with long, stringy auburn hair, prescription tinted glasses, and a mocha complexion. She was somewhat the ugly duckling of the group. She had low-self-esteem and was gullible when it came to the opposite sex. She was also what I like to call user friendly. You know the type. They want you to "do a favor" for them, but it wouldn't be the first time they'd asked. The "favor" always benefits them, but sometimes it's not worth your time, especially when you have other things to do. They're constantly sucking you dry, asking you to drive them places, and basically just using you to their benefit. But she was cool, even for a low-key geek.

I was the tallest of the four. I was 5'7" with a cappuccino complexion and long black hair. They called me the diva of the group, and when the girls were trying to be funny, they called me KD the Diva. That was okay with me because I was not a diva in terms of like some type of bitchy woman ish that has to have her way all the time, or that I was rude and belittled people, or that anyone was beneath me, or that I thought I was all that. I was a diva in how I carried myself and in the way I maintained my beauty, style, and image. I had great style and everyone seem to love my personality because I was confident in who I was. I was able to express my own style and behavior without the influence of others. My character with my friends made me stand out from them. Ultimately, I was the glue that held the group together, somewhat of the leader. I led by example, not by explanation. I was always the calm in the midst of the storm, the one you would call when the chips were down, and I'd be there at the drop of a hat. I never thought I was better than anybody; I just knew I was different than everybody, cut from a different cloth. I was the loyal one, the one you definitely wanted on your team.

Everyone brought something different to the friendship, which made the circle even more engaging, but at the end of the day, loyalty, respect, and integrity were required from everyone. When I was younger, the reason why I chose this group of friends carefully was to ensure they were the ones that could make life better for me and not worse. You see, I trusted them because that is the true basis of any friendship, but these ladies would soon prove that loyalty was a lifestyle none of them could afford, even if it was on sale for 50% off.

3

Ain't None of Your Friends' Business

I never expected us to stay the same people we were in high school, but it seemed like our lives had definitely changed right after we graduated from high school. After high school, Sage decided she had enough of school. She ended up getting hooked up with a good county job by one of her cousins. Chloe, Talia, and I had gone to four year colleges to get our bachelor's degrees. Emil had enrolled in Joe Blasco Makeup School to become a professional makeup artist. Our lives were definitely going in different directions, but we were maintaining the friendship.

After college, Chloe turned into what you might call the "wild child". She was already loud, outspoken, and a hothead. On top of that, her mouth was reckless. She would get into crazy, senseless arguments with us and say things that were over the top or that weren't warranted, which would sometimes end up in a mini fall-out with us and get her into trouble. Even with her crazy antics, we were still able to remain friends. However, all that changed when she started dating Dylan, a coworker from my job.

After college, Chloe wasn't really doing too much with herself. Her parents had money so she wasn't in a rush to utilize her degree. She had a lot of free time on her hands to do pretty much nothing. She came up to my job one day to have lunch with me.

As we sat there eating, I noticed her staring across the room. I said, "Who do you keep looking at?"

She answered, "Some guy who keeps winking at me."

So I turned around to see who she was talking about, then turned back around to eat my food. "Ugh, that's Dylan."

She said, "You know him?"

"Not really."

"Why did you say 'ugh' then?"

I laughed. "Because he looks like the bottom of my damn shoe!"

"You don't think he's cute?" she asked.

I shrugged. "I guess if you like a man who reminds you of a burnt up Cabbage Patch Kid, then sure."

"He's not that bad-looking, Kennedee."

"Well, he's not my type - not that I have a type, but if I did, he wouldn't be it."

Dylan finally made his way over to our table. "Hey, Kennedee. How are you today?" he asked.

"Fine."

"So who's your friend?"

When he said that, I looked over to introduce Chloe, and there she was looking all flustered like Brian McKnight had just walked up to the table. She looked like a sprung chicken already sitting there waiting for me to introduce them. Reluctantly, I said, "Dylan, this is my friend Chloe, and Chloe, this is just some guy that works here named Dylan."

"Some guy?" he huffed. "I'm actually the IT guy for the computer department."

"Oh, is that what you do?" I asked sarcastically. I mean, really, no one was checking for the IT guy.

As he sat down uninvited at our table, he said, "Chloe? What a beautiful name for a beautiful girl."

I turned and looked at him like, for real? I knew he was whack. Ugh!

She said, "Thank you," and she blushed in embarrassment.

He asked, "So how long have you and Kennedee known each other?"

"For almost eleven years now," she replied.

"Wow! That's a long time to be friends with someone so evil."

"Excuse me?" I interjected.

"Well, you're not the nicest person, Kennedee."

"Really?" I asked. "And why is that?"

"Because I say hello when I see you, and you always just wave."

Yep, he was telling the truth, and I was only that way with him because I knew if I was nice to him, it would give him a glimpse of hope that he had a chance to mack me up one day - which was never, ever happening.

Chloe interrupted by saying, "Don't pay her no mind, she's a sweetie pie, you just have to get to know her."

"Well, I'd like to get to know you instead," he said. "I bet you're a sweetie too."

I rolled my eyes in the back of my head with disgust and started shaking my head. This couldn't be happening!

He continued, "So do you think maybe I could call and take you out sometime?"

"Sure!" Chloe said excitedly.

I thought to myself, *This boy ain't even fine...yuck!* I sat there mortified as they exchanged numbers. I was so disgusted that I almost threw up in my mouth. Don't get me wrong, Chloe was a pretty girl, but she was skinny as a pole and flat-chested. At least those bad teeth had finally gotten some braces. Even though we were in our 20's, she still hadn't developed her womanly shape. I guess someone finally showing her some attention was better than nothing.

The next day when I heard from Chloe, she was all thrilled that Dylan wanted to take her out for the weekend. I sat on the other line, not astonished that she was even giving him the time of day. Chloe and Dylan started to date. I only hoped it would work out. I did not want to end up in the middle of some drama, since I was the one who had "introduced" them. Things were going okay until I saw some other girl pick Dylan up from work. I had seen her pick him up before, but I guess I didn't really pay attention because there was no reason to. I asked a co-worker who happened to be coming out as Dylan got in the car if he knew who the Filipino girl picking him up was.

He said, "That's his girl."

"His girl?" I echoed, surprised.

He said, "I think they been together for like four years. Why, you want Dylan or something?"

"Hell no!" I said with a frown, and then I walked away. I chucked as I thought to myself, *Shoot, ain't nobody checking for no Dylan. Well, maybe just that Filipino girl and Chloe.* But I definitely wasn't. I knew this romance would be over soon when I told Chloe that he had a girlfriend.

Being the good friend that I was, I decided to immediately inform Chloe of the situation. I drove

24

over to Chloe's house. I rang the doorbell, and when she came to the door, I told her to come outside for a second. I sat on the hood of my car as Chloe took a seat on the curb.

"What's up, KD?"

"I have something to tell you about Dylan."

"What about Dylan?"

"Well, look, I don't want you to think that I'm trying to be a playa hater, but I don't think you need to be talking to him."

"Why? Because he repulses you?" she asked.

"That, amongst other things, but to top it all off, you don't need to talk to him because I saw some Filipino girl pick him up from work today."

"All of a sudden you see him getting picked up by a girl?" she asked sarcastically.

I was a bit confused because she said it like she didn't believe me. "Yes, I did."

"So the whole time he's been working there you have never seen this girl?"

"Maybe I have, maybe I haven't. To be honest, I was never paying him any attention to begin with until you started talking to him."

All of a sudden she seemed to become mad at me. She got up from the curb and frowned as she dusted herself off, and she didn't say a word. She started walking back towards the house. With her back turned, she said, "I am going to ask him myself about this."

I yelled as I got in the car, "Go ahead, and good luck getting the truth from him! You know these men will lie until they're caught red-handed!"

The next day after work I was walking to my car in the parking lot when I heard the sound of someone running towards me. When I looked back to see it who it was, I saw Dylan coming my way.

"Hey Kennedee!" he yelled while still running. "Hold up for a second!"

I kept walking and said, "What do you want with me, you scandalous dog?"

He grabbed me by the shoulder. "I said hold up!" he demanded.

"Who think you grabbing on like that?" I asked.

He stepped closer. I could feel his hot-ass breath on my face as he whispered, "You need to stay out of my business." Then he grabbed me by the tip end of my nose and said, "Stop being so nosy, bitch!"

Oh lawdy! Did this boy just put his hands on me? My fighter instinct immediately kicked in, but I had to remember I was still at work. I immediately smacked his hand down off of my nose, and as he backed away, I said, "Don't you ever put your hands on me again, punk!"

He stepped back closer to me and asked, "Or you will do what?"

I leaned closer in and said, "Trust me; you don't want to find out!"

"Well, you just remember what I said."

I laughed devilishly and said, "Naw, punk, you better remember what I just said."

After he walked off I stood there, startled that this had just happened to me at work in the parking lot. Pure craziness! This wasn't my man or my problem, but yet I was still in the mix. I was mad as hell as I drove over to Chloe's house for the second day in a row. I was thinking about how this li'l imp had just put his hands on me. I boiled with heat, wishing I hadn't been at work so I could've slapped the ish out of him. I couldn't wait to get to her house to tell her what he did.

When Chloe came to the door, I said, "Why did you have to go and put me in this?"

"He asked me who told me about that other girl, and it wasn't like he didn't know it was you anyway."

"The point is, now you have me mixed up in this drama when I really don't have anything to do with this. Man, I gotta work with this crazo. This man just put his hands on me. You know I don't play that. This ain't cool."

"What? He put his hands on you?" she asked in shock.

"Yeah," I replied.

"Put his hands on you like how?"

I said, "He grabbed my nose and told me to stop being nosy." Why did she start laughing? I fumed, "You think this is funny? Like this is not funny to me. I don't do drama at work, and I knew this was going to happen."

She said, "I am not laughing because he did that. I'm laughing because he don't know who the hell he is messing with."

"You see what I'm saying?" I agreed. "I wanted to slap the shit out of him, but I had to remember I was at work. So what did he say about the girlfriend?"

"He said you were lying."

"What?" I asked, even though I had expected that he would do that.

"Uh huh, he said you're lying."

"So you believe him?"

"I don't know what to believe."

"I've been your homegirl for a minute. You are going to trust him over me?"

"This is the first time a man has paid me this much attention. Who cares if he has a girlfriend?"

"So basically you don't care, right?" I prodded. She didn't say anything. I said, "Well, just let me know now if you don't care that he got a girl and I will just leave the situation alone."

"Well..." She paused. "He's going to be my first."

"Your first what?"

"My first. I want to give him my virginity."

"Have you lost your rabbit-ass mind?" I exploded. "Don't be stupid! You don't even know him! You shouldn't be giving him the time of the day, let along your virginity. It's one thing to keep talking to his black ass knowing he got a girlfriend, but a whole different story when you want to give up something so sacred to someone you don't even know, and, on top of that, you know he got a girl." She was just being plain ole foolish. She stood with her arms crossed and didn't say a word. I threw my hands in the air and said, "Fine then, do what you want, but don't call me when this all comes crashing down."

I didn't hear from Chloe for weeks. Sage called to let me know that Chloe had been in a car accident. Chloe had allowed Dylan to drive her mom's semi-new Mustang while he was drunk. Chloe was taking the blame as the one who crashed the car.

I immediately got a headache. I got off the phone with Sage and called Chloe. When she picked up, I asked her how she was doing because I heard what happened.

"Is big mouth Sage how you found out?"

"Of course! No one tells it better."

"She gets on my nerves, always telling everyone's business!" she huffed.

I asked if she needed anything, but she said she was fine. "So are you going to continue to talk to Dylan?"

"Yes, I love him."

"Huh? You what?"

"I love him," she repeated.

I buried my head in my hand in disbelief that this girl thought she was in love with this man. I asked, "Did you have sex with him already?" The phone was silent for a minute. I finally yelled, "Chloe!"

She whispered, "Yeah."

"Why would you do that? Didn't I tell your ass that he has a girlfriend?"

"Here we go!" she started. But then her angry tone settled down for a second and she said, "Hey Kennedee. I need you to do me a favor."

"What's that?"

"I think I know where his girl stays. Do you think that you could go slash her tires for me?"

"Excuse me? You want me to do what?" I asked.

"Did I stutter? Can you go over there and slash her tires?"

"Huh? No ma'am, I won't. That's your man; therefore it's your problem. I will ride with you, but you want the work done, you put it in yourself. What I look like slashing this chick's tires and I ain't got nothing to do with this situation? You making some bad moves, girly, and I'm not going to be a part of that."

"Hold up," she said. "So now you wanna get all diva-like on me? C'mon now, after all that shit you've done? Now you wanna act like KD the Diva too good to do this?"

I said, "Honey, I put in my own work. I've never asked anyone to do something I wouldn't do for them. "

She took a deep sigh and then said, "Fuck you then!" and hung up the phone.

I sat there looking at the receiver like *Oh no she didn't just hang up on me!* My first thought was to hit redial, but instead I just hung up the phone. I hoped this girl would come to her senses really soon.

A few weeks passed and I hadn't spoken with Chloe, but I heard from Sage that Dylan's real girlfriend had busted Chloe and Dylan coming out of the movies. The girlfriend appeared out of nowhere at the movie theater, jumped out of her car, and stood up on the curb yelling, "That's my man!"

Becoming angry as usual, Chloe had yelled back, "He's my man!"

The two got into each other's faces. Chloe threatened the girl by shouting, "I am going to kick your ass!"

That's when the girl drew back with a closed fist, delivering a blow to the front of Chloe's mouth. As usual Chloe mouth had gotten her into trouble...literally. The fight was broken up when Dylan pulled his girlfriend off of Chloe. Dylan ended up leaving with the girlfriend. Sage said that was why Chloe had to call me for a ride.

"Aw, damn! So not only did she end up in a fight with this girl, but he left Chloe there? Like that should have spoken volumes about this dude!"

Sage said, "When I picked her up, her mouth was bleeding badly because her braces had cut the inside of her mouth."

"Wow! Let me go; I need to call her." I immediately got off the phone with Sage and called Chloe. The phone rang a few times, but there was no answer. So I called back again, still no answer. I thought the third time would be the charm. Well, I guess I was right.

When Chloe answered, she yelled, "I see you calling, bitch! Don't call me ever again!" Then she hung the phone up. I raised an eyebrow when she said "bitch". I knew it must be serious if she was going there with that word.

I called Sage back and explained to her what happened. Apparently, Sage had left out the part of the story where Chloe was blaming me for this whole mess. I said, "Please stop the madness! You can't be serious."

"In her mind, you should have stopped her from talking to Dylan."

I screamed, "What! No ma'am, I will not be the scapegoat for her bad decisions. You know I tried to tell that girl not to mess with that fool, and she didn't listen." I was baffled. I couldn't understand how I wound up getting in the midst of this drama when I had tried my best to stop it before it began.

The next day I heard the doorbell ring. I peeped out the window to see that it was Chloe. I thought to myself, *Cool, she here cuz she came to her senses.*

Wrong! As soon as she saw me at the window, she began to yell, "I see you, bitch, open the door!" Of course she could see me! I had the blinds wide open, peeping my big head out. Thinking back, I should've just kept the door closed and went about my business. In my mind, even though she was yelling obscenities, I still remembered she was my friend. So I opened the door to be greeted by Chloe with a frowned-up face. I said, "What's up?"

She said, "Come outside."

"You can come in."

"Nah, I want you to come outside."

"For what?"

"You heard me, bitch, come outside so I can whip your ass!"

My hearing is not the best so I thought maybe I had misunderstood her. I said, "So you can do what?"

"You heard me! I'm going to whip your ass, bitch!"

"Be careful with the bullets you shooting out your gun and the words you spit out your mouth, because clearly I am the only one thinking logically right now," I cautioned her. "So help me understand, why am I to blame and why are you so mad at me?"

"Because you knew!"

"And I told you, so what's your problem?"

Chloe started yelling at the top of her lungs, "He gave me trichomoniasis thanks to you!"

"Thanks to me?" I asked. "What the hell is trichomoniasis? Help me to help you so I can understand why you are so mad at me."

"Bitch, it don't even matter, just know I got it. And yes, you did do this. I'm going to fuck you up, you dumb bitch!"

"I haven't done anything to you to have you on my porch acting a fool. You're mad at the wrong person, darling. You act like I'm the one who slept with him, gave him whatever this trichomoniasis is, and passed it to you. I have absolutely nothing - nothing - to do with this. I tried to warn you about him, but oh no, you didn't want to listen. You was so in love. Now you're on my porch jumping rough and tough with me. Oh no, honey, it don't work like that." You know, sometimes being the bigger person means not responding to every small, petty insult that gets tossed your way. Sometimes you gotta just leave the petty shit to those petty bitches, and that's exactly what I did when I decided to close that door.

However, when I went to close my door, Chloe then kicked the door with her foot, causing the door to hit me in the face. My forehead instantly started to throb with pain. I grasped my hand over my forehead to try and stop it. I shook my head, trying to warrant it off. I became infuriated as I saw Chloe cowardly walking backwards after she realized what she did.

As I widened the door to go outside on the porch, I yelled, "You hit me in my damn face, you crazy bitch! That's your ass now!" I rushed toward her and took my right hand to face palm her while shoving her into the pillar on the porch. She fell backwards into the bushes. I said, "Do yourself a favor and stay down, bitch!" Yep, shit just got real when I decided to call her a bitch.

As she lay on the ground, my foot stretched back to kick her while she was down. But a voice of reason came over me. I stopped. Yep, that's all I did. Did I feel like fucking her up after all that? Hell yeah! Why didn't I? Because Chloe was my friend. I couldn't fathom the idea of fighting her. She was only angry at me because she didn't have the backbone to be mad at the true villain, which was Dylan. I would not take the blame for none of this, not even her getting cooties from him. That's crazy!

At that moment, I wasn't really sure what direction we were going in, but I truly held my friendships to heart because at the end of the day, real friends were hard to come by. So sometimes you have to pick your battles wisely, because a battle can sometimes turn into war. And trust me; she didn't want to go to war with me. She had just landed her ass in the last seat of the nosebleed section at the KD-and-them game. If she wasn't friends with me, she sure as hell couldn't still be kicking it in the confines of the group. I don't forgive or forget. I just keep it moving...and hopefully the next time I see you, you on some different ish.

4

Secret Lovers

I can't front. Even though Chloe and I weren't rolling with each other anymore, I still felt a little sad that we had fallen out, and I somewhat missed her. But as Mama always said, one monkey don't stop no show. So now the crew consisted of Sage, Talia, and Emil. They say it's bad to mix business with pleasure, blood with business, but no one ever said anything about love with friendships.

Emil had turned out to be even more gorgeous as we began to blossom into womanhood. She had learned at school how to master wearing her makeup flawlessly. She upgraded herself with some fake eyelashes from the beauty supply store. She could bat those fake, store-bought eyelashes, flash that smile, and twirl that hair and guys would fall under her spell.

Emil had been dating Sage's older brother Stefon since our senior year even though Stefon was two years older than us. Sage wasn't too fond of Emil because she liked to flirt a lot even in Sage's presence when we would be out at the club. Emil would always say there was no harm in flirting as long as it didn't go any further, but Sage begged to differ. The rest of us ignored it and downplayed it as her being self-absorbed and needing to steal the spotlight from everyone.

One day Sage, Emil, and I were coming back from dinner. I was dropping Sage off, but I asked her to let me come in for a second to tinkle. Instead of leaving right after my bathroom stop, I imposed and asked to stay so that Emil could kick it with Stefon for a minute. While sitting there conversing with Sage, the doorbell rang. Stefon hopped up to see who was at the door, and when he opened it, we saw that it was Sage's boo Logan. We had all met Logan previously because they had been dating for quite some time. But we hadn't seen him in a while, and when he strolled through the door there was an undeniable swag he had about himself. He even smelled different. He was wearing some manly cologne that made you want to sniff him all night long. I don't know what it was about him that night; maybe we were all growing up and coming into our own. But whatever it was, he sure had the attention of Emil.

I watched Emil as she watched him come from the front door to kiss Sage and to sit down. She seemed infatuated by him all of a sudden. As he sat down, he said hello to everyone. That opened the floodgate for Emil to start chopping it up with him. I sat there peeved as I saw Emil openly throw herself at Logan. She was sitting there twirling the cowlicks in the back of her head with her finger, batting those damn fake eyelashes, giggling at ish that wasn't even funny, and clinging to his every word.

I had finally had enough. I stood up and grabbed my purse and said, "I'm out. Emil, you need a ride or can Stefon drop you off?"

Stefon said, "I got her. Don't worry."

"Y'all have a good night," I said as I left.

On the way home, I thought about how tacky it was to watch Emil engage in such behavior, but there was always something I couldn't put my finger on about her. Maybe this was it.

I waited until the next day to call Sage. When I got Sage on the phone, I didn't have to bring up the topic because she was already on it.

"Yeah, girl, did you see Emil last night trying to flirt with Logan?" she asked.

"Yeah, I thought I was tripping!"

"I saw it all, and I hope Stefon saw it too."

"Girl, that is our girl, and there is no way in hell that she would do something like that to hurt you."

Sage asked, "You think so?"

"Darling, I know so. We've been tight for too long for her to do something like that. She knows better."

"Girl, you right, I'm tripping," Sage agreed.

But to be honest, Sage wasn't tripping. I lied to diffuse the situation. I saw everything and was baffled that this heffa had the gall to do it so shamelessly. In the back of my mind, I only hoped that Emil was just doing her harmless flirting as usual.

I always hosted an annual winter holiday party at my house a week before Christmas. I'd invite all the girls and their significant others. Everyone was there: Stefon and Emil, Sage and Logan, and Talia. We always had a good time when we were all together. However, the atmosphere felt a li'l different this time. It wasn't until Emil started gazing at Logan from across the room that things took a turn for the worse. I was in the kitchen when Talia and Sage walked in.

Sage asked Talia, "Do you see how Emil keeps staring at Logan?"

Talia said, "What's up with that?"

We explained to Talia what had happened a few weeks ago. Talia said, "Hmm, maybe you need to keep an eye on her."

We went out to the patio where the fire pit was going. We were all laughing and sipping on wine. Emil started doing it again. Everything Logan said was funny to her and she was lingering on his every word. Whenever he'd say something funny, she would touch her chest where her exposed cleavage was and snicker.

I kept thinking, *This boy ain't even that funny. Oh my gosh! I wish she would stop with all this fake-ass laughing!*

Then Logan said, "I need my drink refreshed," while holding out his empty glass to Sage.

She said, "I don't know what you looking at me for! You better get it yourself!"

He stood with the glass in his hand, shaking it, saying, "Would anyone else like something?"

Emil said, "Can you just bring out the whole bottle of wine please?"

He said, "Sure," and then proceeded to walk into the house.

Everyone had resumed talking and laughing when all of a sudden Emil got up and said, "Excuse me, I need to go the restroom."

All of us girls looked at each other. Hmm. After about three minutes, I got nosy because I thought one of the two was taking just a li'l too long to come back. So I thought maybe I should see what was taking so long.

When I entered the kitchen, Logan and Emil were chatting it up in the kitchen. They looked alarmed when they saw me.

Logan said, "What's up?"

"It's taking a mighty long time with that wine, and I came to make sure that Emil didn't fall in the toilet."

Emil laughed nervously and said, "Girl, how could big ole me fall in the toilet? You so crazy!" She was sliding by me to get out of the kitchen.

I looked at Logan sideways. He said, "Uh, man, that was her in here asking me what kind of wine I like, that's it."

I said, "You know that ain't cool, right?"

"I promise I would never do anything to jeopardize my relationship with Sage," he protested.

"I hope not, because there will be no disloyalty allowed in this group."

He said, "I got you; I only want to do right by Sage."

"That's good to know, cuz I don't want ya cheating on her. Then I'd have to help her beat your ass." I chuckled, but little did he know I was serious as hell.

When I walked back out to the patio, there seemed to be an awkwardness that ended the party earlier than I anticipated. After the party, I got a late night phone call from Sage asking what happened when I went into the house, so I told her.

She said, "I really hope Emil wouldn't do me or my brother dirty like that."

"Well, I hope she would respect the code, but you can't worry about what-ifs. What's done in the dark will come to light," I replied.

"I hope so! Good night."

It was a couple of days before Christmas when all of us girls decided to do some last minute shopping.

We met at Sage's house to carpool to the mall. We hit a couple of stores and were in and out. We grabbed a bite to eat at the Cheesecake Factory and made our way back home. When we got back to the house, we all hurried to get in the car because it had started to pour down rain. Sage didn't get out of her car because she said she needed to run to the grocery store.

We all went our respective ways. About an hour later, my phone kept ringing. I saw that it was Talia, but I was busy wrapping gifts so I decided I'd just call her back when I was done. About five minutes later the phone was ringing again. This time it was Sage. I thought to myself, *she's going to have to wait too.* Then right after the phone stopped ringing, it started ringing again, and once again it was Sage. I was thinking, *Man, what the hell is so important?* So finally I answered. I said, "Yes, darling, how can I help you?"

Instead of hearing Sage say hello, all I could hear was Talia and Sage talking. Apparently I was on a three-way call. I yelled, "Hello!"

Sage said, "Kennedee, you there"

"Yes. What's so important?"

Sage began, "You will never, ever guess what happened!"

"What? Girl, hurry up, I gotta finish wrapping these gifts."

She asked, "Can y'all come back over real quick?"

I said, "What's so important that we need to come out of this house when it's pouring cats and dogs?"

Sage answered, "Emil left something in my car and I have some things to show you."

We both said we were on our way.

I put on my coat and grabbed my umbrella. On the way there, I said, "Sweet baby Jesus, I hope Sage ain't found out Logan and Emil is messing around, cuz I know that's at least the vibe I got that night." I knew all hell would break loose if this was the case. We had all been friends for years and that would be devastating to the circle if Emil did what I thought she did.

I arrived at the same time as Talia and we both walked to the door together. While we were waiting for the door to be answered, Talia turned to me and said, "KD, do you think Emil cheated with Logan?"

Before I could answer, Sage was opening the door. I looked at Talia and said, "I guess we about to find out."

When I walked in the door, Sage made her way over to the couch to have to a seat, and Stefon was pacing the floor. I whispered to Talia, "This can't be good! Look at Stefon wearing a hole in that floor."

I went and sat down next to Sage on the couch and asked, "So what's up? You going to tell me what the hell is going on?"

She asked, "You don't want to wait until Emil gets here?"

Sage jumped off the couch to go in her pocket. She pulled out a two-way pager. Sage said, "Look what this bitch left in my car!"

Clearly it was Emil's; you could tell by the case. I threw my hands up and said, "Man, what's up? Will you hurry up and get to it? I need to get back home."

Sage came back to the couch and said, "Scoot over." She sat between Talia and I on the couch. Sage began to scroll through the messages. She got to a familiar name, but it was a name that probably shouldn't have been in Emil's two way. Emil had been two-waying Martel, which was Stefon's and Sage's cousin. Hell, I don't know what was worse, expecting to see evidence of cheating with Logan, or finding out that Emil was hitting up Martel several times a day. The messages showed the same from Martel.

Sage said, "I called Emil on her house phone to let her know I had her two way. She said she would be on her way in an hour and jokingly told me not to be reading her messages. It piqued my curiosity so I looked and saw all these messages. That's why I wanted you all to get her before she did, so you guys could read them."

Stefon added, "And I told Martel to come through to scoop me up to go to the club."

I said, "This is going to be a treacherous mess!" I sat there shaking my head. One side of me didn't want to be there to witness all this crashing down, but the "inquisitive" side of me wouldn't allow me to leave. I guess I wanted to see it rather than hear about it later.

All of a sudden the doorbell rang. It felt like time stopped as we sat there frozen, looking to see who had arrived first - Emil or Martel.

Sage hopped off of the couch. "I'll get it."

As soon as she opened the door, there was Emil standing there. "Why everybody cars outside? I thought everybody went home."

Sage said, "Nah, I called everybody and told them to meet back here."

Emil began to make her way to the couch where Stefon was sitting. She went to sit down next to him and he said, "Bitch, don't sit your ass down next to me!"

She leaned over him and said, "Baby, what's wrong?"

"Don't 'baby' me!" Emil went to stroke his face to calm him down, but he slapped her hand down before her hand could reach his face. He said angrily, "Don't you dare put your hands on me, you lying-ass whore!"

Emil looked dazed and confused. "What's going on? What's this all about? Where is my two way?" She looked around at everyone.

Talia and I looked at each other, unsure of who should speak up and say something. Before we were able to say anything, we saw the two-way being twirled in the air by Sage. She said, "Catch this, bitch!"

At that very moment, Emil knew she was busted. She said, "Look, I can explain."

Stefon jumped up and said "What the hell is there to explain? We saw it all in your messages; we seen it all! Now how the hell you going to get out of that?

Ding dong! The doorbell interrupted. Once again, Sage made her way over to the door to answer it.

Martel came in the door saying loudly, "Where Stefon at? We about to get buck wild tonight." As his eyes scanned the room, he saw everyone and asked, "Why everybody looking so serious. Did somebody die?"

Stefon walked over. "Not yet."

That's when Emil said, "He knows," and lowered her head in shame.

Martel went to turn and walk away, but Stefon grabbed him by the collar and snatched him back. Martel turned and swung on Stefon. They both began to deliver fist blows to each other. It was like watching a real boxing match. One would deliver a jab, and the other would take a jab. Finally after a couple of blows, I decided to get off the couch and run in the kitchen where Sage was standing in the doorway, because I didn't want to end up being a casualty. Talia followed my lead.

Emil started screaming, "Break it up, break it up!" and she tried to break the fight apart.

I wasn't willing to break up the fight, but I was a bit surprised when I asked Sage, "Aren't you going to help break up the fight?"

She said, "Hell no!" and continued to watch like it didn't even phase her that her family was fighting like that.

Emil had wedged her way in between the two. Stefon stepped back as if he was done, but Martel reached over Emil's head for another swing at Stefon. Stefon ducked and came ramming himself into Emil and Martel, causing both of them to fall back on the glass-top coffee table. It felt like a fight scene from a movie. We were all standing in the kitchen doorway as glass started flying in the air and we all shielded our faces.

The Aftermath

I finally uncovered my face to see Emil and Martel on the floor. He was bleeding from his head. I immediately started helping Emil up off the floor. Martel was holding his bloody head as he attempted to get up. He was on his knees while grasping for the couch.

Stefon said, "Naw, man, you better go bleed at your own house." Martel got up and staggered his way out the door to his car. Talia and Sage were still standing there in shock. They snapped back into reality with the sound of Stefon's voice yelling as he pointed at Emil. "Grab your shit and get the fuck out my house, Emil!"

While Emil was grabbing her stuff, I started grabbing mine. Shoot, I thought I better leave before they asked for help cleaning up all that glass. Didn't nobody have time for that. Shoot, I still needed to get home. Man, all this drama around the holidays was too much for my taste.

As we made our way outside, I noticed Emil's arm was bleeding. I asked her if she wanted to go to the hospital, but she said she thought she would be okay. "But damn, I broke a nail. Is my face okay?"

"You look fine. Not a scratch," I said.

I asked her, "What were you thinking messing around with Martel, of all people?"

"Remember that week my car wasn't working?"

I said, "Yeah, what about it?"

"Well, one day Stefon couldn't pick me up from work, so he sent Martel. On the way home, he started complimenting me on how nice I looked. When he dropped me off, he asked if he could come in to use the restroom, then it led to him asking if he could stay to see the third quarter of the game. During the game, we were talking, and one thing led to another. Girl, you know how I like to flirt. I just couldn't control myself. Martel is fine. I had to have him. I don't know why everyone is trippin'. It's not like Stefon and I are married or something."

"How long has this been going on?" I asked her.

"About three months."

Before I gave her my lecture, Stefon walked out. "Damn, bitch, you still here? What part of leave don't you understand?"

She turned to me and gave me a hug and said, "I'll call you later."

To be honest, I wasn't sure if Emil was even remorseful, because not once did I see her shed one tear. She was just ashamed she had gotten caught. As I got in the car, I saw Talia walking out. As Talia passed my car, she put up her thumb and pinky finger to motion for me to call her.

I called her as soon as I got to the house. When she picked up, I asked, "What took you so long to leave?"

She said, "Girl, I was in there helping Sage pick up that glass."

I started laughing. I said, "Girl, see, that's why I hurried up and left. I was not helping clean up that mess!"

"I feel you. I should've followed your lead, because now I got a small cut on my finger. So what Emil have to say?"

"Well, it started with him picking her up from work as a favor for Stefon, and they ended up sleeping together."

"Are you serious? How long this been going on?"

"She said about three months."

"You know she needs an ass whipping for that. That's some bullshit! She want to run around flirting with everybody else's man."

I said, "Well, there was no way she was going to tell us that. She knows we would have told Sage, and she definitely would have had to tell Stefon."

"Look, I just walked in the house when you called. Let me get situated," Talia said.

"Okay, I need to finish wrapping these gifts anyway."

Later on that night around midnight, my phone rang. When I looked at the clock and saw how late it was, I knew either someone needed something or someone died. Well, that's the old-time saying. I picked up the phone and I saw that it was Sage's number. I thought, *What the hell is it now?* I picked up the phone while rubbing my eyes, trying to wake myself up. I answered by saying, "This better be important." She didn't say anything. I said, "Hello, are you there?"

"Kennedee, why would Emil do something like this?" Sage asked.

"What?"

"You heard me."

I said, "You know my hearing ain't that great."

"Well, put the phone on the good ear."

"It is on the good ear. Just repeat what you said, please."

"Why would Emil do something like this?" Sage repeated.

"Girl, this couldn't wait 'til the morning?"

She said, "I'm just sitting here thinking. We've all known each other since we were thirteen years old; that's eleven years. That's a long time. I never thought she would pull something like this. Did you?"

"I'm just as surprised as you." I had known Emil's family for years; I had known everyone in the crew families for years. Their family was my family. I was unsure how I was going to mend this situation with these two, but I couldn't fathom the idea of losing two more friends.

I conjured up a brilliant idea to have everyone over for New Year's Eve, but I didn't divulge who was on the guest list. I invited Sage, Talia, and Emil. I secretly invited Emil because I wasn't sure if Sage wanted to see her with everything being so fresh still.

Sage and Talia were the first to arrive, and the emptiness of the house was filled with a few laughs until the doorbell rang. I had invited Emil, but when the rest of the ladies saw her as well as Chloe, the room immediately got cold, quiet, and intense. I said, "Emil, I invited you, not Chloe."

She said, "Chloe wanted to talk to you."

"Talk to me about what?" I asked angrily.

Chloe said, "Well, about everything that went down."

"Please, Kennedee?" pleaded Emil.

I said, "You know what? It's cool. Come on in and y'all have a seat." I was really curious to see what

Chloe had to say a few months later after calming her ass down.

As they copped a seat, Sage said, "Well look who decided to show up: Cain and Abel. But it's hard to decipher which one of you bitches is Cain." She chuckled.

Talia interjected, "I think you have your biblical stories mixed up. I think you're talking about the Prodigal Son."

Sage snapped back, "Does it even really matter? Both of these bitches are traitors."

I interrupted, "Hey, cut it out with all that bitch stuff and let them speak their peace first, and then we can go from there. I asked everyone to come here today because we have all been friends for a very long time. But if you have a problem with someone, now is the time to address it, because if we going to keep rolling together, there can't be no underlying issues. If you got a problem with someone, handle it however you need to. Exposing the problem to everybody is just some straight sucka shit. PERIOD."

The room was quiet for a few seconds. I was looking around at everyone. I said, "Who wants to go first?"

I heard Chloe clear her throat. "I'll go first," she said. "First I'd like to thank Kennedee for having us all over."

I interrupted her. "Hold on, let's be clear. You were not invited; you showed up, and that's a big difference. And to be honest, I really don't appreciate Emil bringing you to my house uninvited. Like really, what the fuck is up with this? The last time I saw you, you were outside that door telling me come outside to get my ass whipped. You remember that, don't you? Because I sure haven't forgotten."

Chloe said, "Look, I know you're still pissed off about what happened a few months ago, but I'm sorry. I was wrapped up in my emotions for being played and I took it out on you when you only had my best interests at heart. You know how I am. Sometimes I react without thinking. I'm truly sorry. Will you please forgive me?"

I sat there rubbing my head, trying to figure out what to say or do. Then I thought about all the good memories we shared from the time we were girls into early womanhood. The good outweighed the bad. So I looked up and said, "What you did hurt me to the core. I could have easily mopped the floor with you, but I remembered you were a friend and not a foe. I can't continue to hold a grudge for someone I did – correction, do – care about. All of you ladies are like sisters to me. I would never want to cause harm to you or see harm done to you."

Chloe's eyes filled up with tears.

I said, "Girl, come over here and get this love." I stood up to greet her with a hug.

She came over and started crying uncontrollably.

All of a sudden I heard Sage say, "Well, isn't this a Hallmark moment? KD the Diva is trying to have a Kumbaya moment with us. Isn't this sweet?" she said sarcastically. "However, I'm no softy like

Kennedee." She slapped her hands on her thick hips.

I said jokingly, "Hold up, ain't nothing soft about me, but my ass. You know how I roll. But seriously, as I look around this room, I see not just a group of friends that I have grown up with, but my fam. That's what we are to one another; that's what you have always been to me. All the good times we've had has to supersede all this bull-ish. Ten plus years, y'all, c'mon."

Sage stood up grabbed her belongings. "I love the loyalty that Kennedee has to this group of folks right here," she said as she waved her hand in the air. "You can't find one more loyal than this one right here." She pointed to me. "But Emil, you, on the other hand, you're foul, sneaky, and conniving.

And Chloe, I don't even know what the fuck you're doing here. You were like seriously angry with Kennedee over a situation she tried to warn you about, and then you had the nerve to try to fight her? Bitch, please! Get the fuck outta here with them fake-ass crocodile tears. You know one thing we've always had in this circle was loyalty. Loyalty ain't a learned or acquired behavior; it's either in you or it's not. And it's not in either of you." As she made her way to open the door, she looked back and added, "For the record, I'm cool with everyone in this room except for Emil and Chloe." She slammed the door behind her on the way out.

I said, "Emil, you don't want to maybe stop her to try and apologize?"

She said, "For what? I was fucking her brother not her."

I just sat there a little dumbfounded as she sat there still unremorseful. She showed no empathy. It kinda felt like the season finale of the *Housewives of Atlanta* where all the women come together and pretend like they're going to mend things, but instead it turns into the brawl for it all.

My intentions were good, but thinking back, I don't think that was a good idea to arrange that meeting with emotions still running high. Once again, there was division in the circle, so there it was. If Sage was going, Emil and Chloe weren't going, and if Emil and Chloe were going, Sage wasn't going. Talk about awkwardness! But I had to respect how they felt about one another. As far as Chloe, I let her back in the circle, but I'd learn later that when folks

wanna jump ship with no reason and then try to

swim back with an excuse, it was better to keep the

boat moving without them. Chloe would soon

prove she had changed, but for the worst.

6

Age Ain't Nothing but a Number

My family has always bred some nice-looking men and my li'l cousin Dallas was no exception. He was honey brown with black, wavy hair, and dimples when he smiled. He was very charismatic. He was only fifteen years old, but he was already 6'4", which made him appear older than what he seemed, but when he opened that mouth to try and spit game, it was apparent that he was still a child. He would try to flirt with the girls whenever I had him over or at holiday functions. His favorite line to tell Sage was, "Girl, you thicker than a Snickers. When you going to let me get them digits?" Or he'd tell

Emil, "Are you a parking ticket? 'Cause you've got fine written all over you." His line for Talia was,

"Just call me milk; I'll do your body good." And for Chloe, he'd say, "Girl, you must be a light switch, cuz every time I see you, you turn me on!" His lines were corny as hell, but we would usually laugh it off. It was harmless because I knew my friends had enough sense to know that he was still a kid.

One summer Dallas's parents were going on vacation. They asked if it would be okay if he stayed with me for a few weeks. Other than him always bumping the newest rap lyrics to the top of the ceiling and having a bottomless stomach, he was a pretty good kid. I figured sure, it wouldn't be a problem, and besides, he was my favorite cousin. It would be nice to have him spend some time with me.

Even though Dallas was there, I still went about my regular routine of going to work and going home. The first weekend he was with me, I decided that he was responsible enough to stay at the house by himself. I called up the girls and asked them if they felt like having a girls' night out. Chloe and Emil met at my house and we went and ate dinner in Century City, followed by a relaxed atmosphere at a club in the Marina.

When we arrived back at the house, all the lights were out. I thought it was unusual for a teenager to be asleep at 1 a.m. on a summer night. As soon as we hit the door, we smelled sex in the air.

Emil said, "Mmm, smell like somebody been fucking."

I looked around and on my couch there was a girl's jacket and purse. I picked up the purse by my index finger. "Looks like I have an extra houseguest." I put my index finger over my lips so they would know to be quiet. I quietly slipped into the kitchen, let the cold water run slow, and ran the water until it was nice and cold. I got a pitcher and placed a few ice cubes in it just to make sure it was extra cold.

Chloe asked, "What are you going to do with that?"

I said, "Y'all come with me." I began to tiptoe to my second bedroom where I could smell my candles burning and hear the sounds of R. Kelly's "Bump and Grind". I thought, How appropriate! I heard moaning and groaning coming from the room. I hurriedly opened the door. I shouted, "Ya li'l nasty ass!" I threw the ice cold water on Dallas and some butt-naked girl grinding on top of him.

I could hear the girls standing in the doorway busting up laughing. As the young girl got up, she yelled, "Who the fuck are you?"

Before I could answer, Chloe made her way into the room, yelling, "Who the fuck are you, li'l bitch?"

I scratched my head because it seemed to me that Chloe was overreacting just a tad. I mean, after all, it wasn't like Dallas was her cousin. I didn't know why she got so mad at the girl.

Chloe got in the girl's face, saying "Who are you? Who are you?"

The girl seemed scared, so I grabbed Chloe by the arm and told her she needed to calm down. I said to the stranger, "Look, li'l girl, I'm his cousin and this is my house and my bed you're in. I suggest you put your clothes on and see your way out of my house before I call ya mama and let her know what you were over here doing. Dallas, get your dumb ass up and get the mop and get this water off my hardwood floors, and make sure you change the linen with ya nasty self. You get on my nerves." I was so disgusted and disappointed with him.

I sat in the living room with the girls as we waited for the young lady to exit the room. She said, "I'm sorry, ma'am. I didn't know this was your house."

"Oh, because you thought this was his parents' house it was okay?"

She said, "No, I thought this was his place."

I laughed. "Why in the devil would a fifteen-year-old have his own place?"

"What? He's fifteen?"

I said, "Yes, darling, fifteen. How old did he tell you he was? Before you answer that, how old are you?"

"I'm nineteen," she answered.

The girls and I said all at the same time, "Nineteen!"

I yelled, "Dallas, get your black self out here!"

He came out with nothing but his basketball shorts on with his fake LL Cool J chest all exposed like someone wanted to see that. I said, "Boy, go put on a shirt, ain't nobody trying to see all of that right now."

He ran back in the room, threw on a wife beater, and came back in. I said, "So, li'l Romeo, you telling lies now? Tell her how old you really are."

"I'm fifteen," he said meekly.

"I am so sorry, honestly, I didn't know," the girl apologized.

I said, "Well, since you do now, I can expect for you to lose his number. Right?"

"Not a problem." She grabbed her stuff and walked out the door.

I turned to Dallas and said, "What were you thinking? Don't even bother answering, because you weren't thinking, boy. You do not use my house for this type of shit. Man, I can't even look at you right now. Just go clean up that room." As he walked down the hallway, I yelled, "You need to start thinking with your big head instead of your little head!"

He turned around with a stupid look and said, "What does that mean?"

"See, that's the reason why you ain't supposed to be fucking. You don't even know the difference. You too in a hurry to grow up. You need to slow down before you end up catching something you can't get rid of."

I went and sat on the couch. Emil said, "You know you sound like somebody's mama."

"Naw, he already got one of those. I'm trying to be the voice of reason."

"Kennedee, you are so right."

Chloe interrupted and said, "I can't believe him, I just really can't believe him! That boy is something else." She jumped up. "He is a piece of work!" She stormed out the door.

I looked dumbfounded as Emil said, "What's her problem?"

I said, "I don't know, but you know how she can be, always riding high on emotions. She still gets on my nerves with that. Let me go in here and make sure he is getting this room together. I'll talk with you later. Let yourself out."

That was week one of his three-week stay. Week two I didn't go anywhere but to work, and I stayed home that weekend to make sure he didn't do anything else stupid. However, I did have Emil and Chloe over for a dip in the pool. I allowed him to

have a friend over to keep him company and to keep
his usual flirting with the girls down to a minimum,
so he invited over one of his friends. I remember
none of the girls really wanted to get in the pool cuz
nobody wanted to get their hair wet. Go figure!
Instead we sat on the edge of the pool with our legs
dangling in the beautiful indigo blue water. The
girls finally wanted to get out and sit at a table by
the pool. They were sipping on some wine and
nibbling on some yummy treats.

All of a sudden I saw Dallas sneaking up behind
Chloe's chair. Before I could stop him, he had
grabbed her and was heading for the pool. All I
could do was yell, "No!" as the water splashed up,
hitting all of us - including our hair. Everyone got

up yelling. As Dallas came up from the water along with Chloe, we could hear her fussing.

When Chloe got out of the pool, it was apparent that she was upset with Dallas. She said, "I can't believe you'd do that! You are such a jerk!" Dallas made his way over to where she was standing. He began to apologize. She interrupted by saying, "You are such an asshole! I hate you! Just get away from me! I don't want to see your stupid face right now!"

Dallas attempted to make the situation better by reaching in for a hug, but Chloe pushed him away. Then she came to the table and said, "Give me the keys to the house. I need to get my stuff so I can leave."

I reached the keys out to her and she snatched them and stormed off. Emil asked, "Is it me, or is she overreacting?"

"Naw, she overacting as usual," I agreed.

Chloe returned shortly with the keys. I asked, "So you're going to leave?"

"Yes! He gets on my nerves! He's always doing something stupid."

I said, "Well, I'm really sorry he threw you in the pool."

"Uh huh," she said as she walked off.

I just brushed it off as one of her usual crazy blow-up moments. She couldn't control that hot head of hers, and she was always throwing some type of crazy tantrum that no one could relate to.

Finally week three arrived. Dallas's parents would be returning soon. Not that I didn't enjoy having my favorite li'l cousin over, but there was a reason why I didn't have any children. I didn't have time to be responsible for anyone else. A few nights before his parents were scheduled to return, Dallas and I went to Olive Garden for dinner. Any time I'd patronize the Olive Garden I would order my favorite soup, the Toscana, even though my stomach wouldn't always agree with it. That night Dallas and I ate until our bellies were about to bust. By the time we returned home, we were food drunk and we both turned in early. I went to work the next day, however, after getting to work I felt ill. I had to leave early because the soup from the night before started giving me stomach problems.

I was hoping to come home to some peace and quiet since I wasn't feeling well. When I walked in the house, I scanned the house for signs of Dallas. Under normal circumstances, I would've paged him, but my stomach was hurting so bad I thought that he must've found something to do, so I unlocked my room and went to lay down in my bed.

I must've dozed off because I was awakened by the sound of knocking and rumbling. So much for getting some rest! I sighed heavily as I got out of the bed to see what in the world was going on. As I opened my room door, I could hear loud moaning and groaning. I rolled my eyes. "Not this ish again!"

Before I opened the door, a thought hit me. I went back in my room and got my baseball bat. My idea was that I was going to scare the mess out of this boy. As I opened the door I commenced to screaming, "Someone is about to receive some real bad injuries!" As I walked in the door, I started to swing the bat in the air. Don't get me wrong, I wasn't going to beat anyone with the bat; I just wanted to scare 'em.

Dallas yelled, "Kennedee, stop, stop!"

Then I heard a familiar voice yell, "Girl, you tripping!"

I hadn't taken the time to see who was underneath Dallas, and to my surprise when I cocked my head sideways to see who it was, there was Chloe naked with her flat-chested self. My heart dropped down to the bottom of my stomach, and not because this was my first time seeing Chloe naked as adults. For a second though, I started thinking, Damn, this heffa ain't got no titties. It was because my good friend had crossed the line with my underage cousin. I was lost in disgust.

I was snapped out of my trance when Chloe yelled, "Bitch, what the fuck are you staring at? Will you just hand me my clothes?" she demanded.

At that very moment it dawned on me that my twenty-five-year old friend was sexing my fifteen-year-old cousin. I went berserk. I started yelling, "Get the hell out of my house!" I started swinging that bat now with the intent to hurt. As I swung the bat in the area of the bed, Dallas quickly jumped up and fled. Chloe must have thought I was playing, so I swung again, and this time I hit the bedroom window, shattering the glass. Chloe hopped up, dusting small pieces of glass from her naked boy-shaped body.

She said, "You know you crazy, bitch!"

"I'm crazy? I'm crazy? You're the one laid up here with my fifteen-year-old cousin! He's fifteen...fifteen! You have about ten seconds to get your ish and get out."

"Or you're going to do what?"

I took a long, deep breath and exhaled. I begin to count. "10, 9, 8, 7, 6, 5, 4, 3..."

By the time I got to 2, she said, "Okay, okay! Dang, just let me get dressed."

I walked out of the room, and about two minutes later she came out. I could see her peep her head around the corner as she came to the end of the hallway. She said, "Kennedee, are you mad?"

I got up and started to walk to the front door as she still stood at the end of the hallway. "You gotta go," I said as I pointed to the door.

As she started walking past me, she asked again, "Kennedee, are you mad?"

I just looked at her because she already knew the answer to her nitwitted question. As she walked out the door she looked back and said, "Fine then, bitch, be like that!"

I don't know, but at that moment, I snapped. I grabbed her by the hair with my hand and pulled her back into the house, then slammed her against the wall. I began to place my hand around her throat. "I don't know, Chloe, you tell me if I'm mad. What? I can't hear you. Am I mad?" Of course she couldn't answer; my hand was around her throat. Instead she started gasping for air.

I flung my hand down and let her go. "What kind of friend are you? I trusted you, you dirty, filthy, nasty tramp!" I know dirty, filthy and nasty all had the same meanings, but that's how badly I wanted her to know how low-down she was for sleeping with my li'l cousin. As much as I wanted to put my hands all over her, I couldn't. The friend in me wouldn't allow myself to go there with her. So I just said, "Get the fuck out my house!" She proceeded out the door, and I yelled, "Don't come back here either, and we ain't friends no more!"

As I turned to walk back in the living room, Dallas was standing there in my pink satin robe with the sleeves damn near up to his elbows. I said, "Fool, what are you doing in my robe?"

"I needed to cover up."

"Oh, now you wanna care, oh, now you wanna care? You are sooooooo unbelievable. Boy, if you don't get the hell out of my robe and go put on some damn clothes!" I had a seat on the couch. I couldn't quite gather my thoughts. I had missed all the signs: the day at the pool, the night from the dinner, a few weeks ago at the 4th of July party when I caught them hugging on the side of the house. I asked myself if there were other signs that I had missed. I couldn't worry myself; I could only deal with the present. I wanted to know when it started, for how long, or who initiated it. I could care less about this if he was eighteen at least, but he was a child, and he was my favorite cousin, so the betrayal made the pill a little harder to swallow.

I had to figure it all out in three days before his parents got back. I made him give me his pager, his Nintendo, and his CD player so he could have time to reflect on his actions. I was reflecting too. I made a phone call to a friend who happened to be a police officer. I was told that statutory rape occurs when any person twenty-one years of age or older engages in an act of unlawful sexual intercourse with a minor who is under sixteen years of age, and that person is guilty of either a misdemeanor or a felony and could serve up to one year in county jail.

After the phone call I had to determine if I should or shouldn't report it. Dallas's pager began to chime. I picked up the pager to see who it was, and it was Chloe's number. I felt infuriated as I called her.

She picked up by saying, "Hi, baby." Then she whispered, "Is she around?"

"This is she, you nasty bitch! Why the hell are you still contacting my cousin? You know I've been to jail before and don't have no problem going back. Would you like to go back with me?"

She quickly hung up. That was it. I think she had mistaken my kindness for weakness just because I didn't whip her ass like she knew I was truly capable of doing. This had to end I was going to tell his parents so they could press charges.

Then I thought, *Damnnnnnn, that would be so jacked up for her.* If she was found guilty, she go to jail, would be placed in the sex offender's registry and she would be prevented from living or loitering within 1,000 feet of schools, day care centers, parks, etc. Did I really want to turn her life upside down like that? That was the friend in me with that thought trying to rationalize.

I said, "Come on, D."

"Where are we going?"

"We going for a ride."

We jumped in the car and started driving. I said, "Dallas, let me ask you something."

"What?"

"What were you thinking messing around with Chloe?"

He glared out the passenger window and said, "I don't know."

"How long has this been going on?"

"For a month. It started at the 4th of July party at Uncle's house. She was flirting with me, and she asked me for my pager number. At first I thought she was just playing, but she slid me her number so I went ahead and gave her mine. She would hit me up and I'd call back. First it just started off with her coming by when my parents were at work. She would just stop by real quick and suck my dick. Then we started having sex at the park, her car, or at the beach. It was her idea to come over to your house since we thought you were going to be at work."

"Ugh! Shut up! I don't want to hear anymore. My ears are bleeding from this filth." I was totally revolted that this grown-ass woman had been screwing a child.

I arrived at Chloe's house, where she was still living with her parents. Dallas asked, "Who lives here?"

I replied, "Dallas, you don't worry about that. You just stay in the car and don't say a word."

I hit the doorbell and Chloe answered the door. "Oh, it's you. What do you want?"

I said, "Drop the attitude with me, because all that rah-rah shit will get you an ass whipping you don't want. You feel me?"

"What's up, Kennedee?"

"What's up is my cousin is fifteen years old. Do you get it? What part of that don't you understand? He is a child. He only looks like a man, but he is still a boy." When I said "boy", I emphasized it by yelling, which prompted her mom to come see what was going on. I said, "Hi, Mrs. Jackson."

She frowned. "Kennedee, you here to choke out my baby again?"

I retorted, "Did your baby tell you what she did to get choked out?"

"I should call the police on you right now," Mrs. Jackson threatened.

I huffed and said, "Good, then I can make a report on her too."

Chloe started saying, "Mom, just go back in the living room."

"What report?" said Mrs. Jackson, ignoring Chloe.

I said, "So Chloe, you ran home and told her what I did, but not what you did?"

"What did you do, Chloe?" her mother asked her.

"She has been having sexual relations with my fifteen-year-old cousin for a month now."

Her mom yelled, "What!"

"You heard me. Now look here, Chloe, that boy in that car is off limits to you, which means do not see him, do not call him, and do not page him. You are to have no contact with him whatsoever. You get it? You know I don't play police games; I serve my own form of justice. But I swear on my mama, I will come back here with his parents and the police if I

hear you were with him again or contacted him."

I heard the door slam as I walked off, and got in the

car. I told Dallas, "If I hear of you doing anything

with Chloe again, you will leave me no other choice

but to report her to the police and let your mama

and dad know what happened. I'm sure your mom

wouldn't be too thrilled about your li'l escapades at

my house or any of the other stuff you just told me.

Understand?"

"Understood," he said meekly.

After that situation with Dylan and her I should've

known better. But I trusted her; she was my friend.

Where was the loyalty? Where was the trust?

Where was the respect? Apparently it was in my

cousin's pants. Hell, I don't know what her reasoning was, nor did I care to know.

Three months later I heard a knock on the door. When I looked out the peephole, there was Chloe. It didn't faze me one bit not to turn the knob to open the door or allow her back in my life. What apology could she offer this time? How sorry could she be apologizing for something she knew was wrong in the first place? I was good. I didn't need to hear nothing else from her. She had shown her ass one too many times on my watch. She was a hothead when we were young, but she had turned into an unpredictable time bomb now. Like I said before, there are rules to this shit. I just had to turn my back on the friendship, because when it came to my friendships, I didn't have time for all that rah-

rah stuff. I certainly didn't have time to keep going back and forth with her. We were done.

<u>The Only Time You Call</u>

I remember it was like yesterday when Tyson and Talia met. It was summer of 2000 at Venice Beach. Emil, Talia, and I were walking from the boardwalk towards the parking lot when we saw this fine pack of men approaching us. I mean, they was all so fine that it was hard to choose which one I was going to mack up. As they came our way, I started to claim dibs on the one that I wanted. I dodged the pretty boy because somehow I knew he would turn out to be a problem.

The pretty boy, who turned out to be Tyson, ended up talking to Talia. Tyson was fine. He was at least

6'2" with a caramel-brown complexion, pretty hazel eyes, and curly hair, but I think it might have really been an S curl. Either way he was fine. In addition, he was quite charming, and intelligent. He would tell Talia that he'd never met anyone as beautiful as her.

Talia was an assistant bank manager. She was in charge of promoting and marketing the branch and its products, meeting with customers, resolving any problems or complaints, ensuring there was a high level of customer service, monitoring sales targets, and reporting to the head office. She was making decent money. She had always low-key been a geek so I wasn't surprised at her success.

She had come a long way from the ugly duckling she was in junior high. She had what some would say was the body of a goddess, but a face from hell. She finally had gotten some glasses that complimented her face a bit. However, Tyson seemed to really be into her. I was happy for her that she had finally found a good man.

I thought it was true love until he asked her to borrow $400. I don't know about you, but giving/loaning grown men money is not a good look, especially if you've only known him for about twelve weeks. That beefcake must have been hella good, because Talia totally ignored my warning when I told her not to give that boy that money and she did it anyway. She could be so damn gullible when it came to men. When she called me crying about not hearing from him after he got the money, I wasn't nowhere near shocked.

"Do you think you can pick me up?" she asked.

I said, "I'm on my way to church, what's up?"

She suggested, "Why don't you pick me up so you can go with me to this new church?"

"What new church?"

"It's in Inglewood."

"It's new?"

"No, I just haven't been there before," she said.

"Alright, be ready in thirty minutes."

When we got to Faithful Central, she motioned for me to pull into the parking lot. "Park right over there!" she demanded.

I said, "Why everybody look like they coming outta church already?"

"Oh, I think this is the 11:00 service or something letting out."

I found a parking spot, I backed the car into the stall. Talia began to recline the passenger chair. "What are you doing?" I asked as I looked over at her.

"I'm hiding."

"From who? We at a church."

"From Tyson."

"Please tell me that you didn't just make me miss church over some foolishness with y'all two."

"Well, I haven't heard from him, so I figured I'd catch him here."

"Wow, you can't be serious right now! Why did I need to come?"

"Girl, he knows my car. I just want my money back, that's all."

I sat there in disbelief. "We should've just gone to his house. Look, I am not about to act a fool on the church grounds. So you're on your own with this."

"Fine," she huffed.

We were out there for about ten minutes with her in the passenger seat looking like crouching tiger/hidden dragon, thinking she was hiding by slouching down. I looked over to my right side and I had to do a double take. "Oooh!" I shouted.

She popped up in the seat. "What?"

I pointed out the windshield. There was Tyson walking past the car with some other girl, who had evidently worn her too-tight club dress from the night before to church by mistake. Before I could say anything else, I could hear the alert letting me know one of the car doors had been left ajar. I looked over to see my car door wide open with Talia missing from the passenger seat.

It all happened so fast I couldn't even tell you verbatim what happened. All I know is that as soon I looked up, Talia's glasses were sitting on my dashboard and my passenger side door was open. I saw the tight-dress girl with a fist full of Talia's hair. I hurried up and jumped out of the car. All church etiquette went out the window. I yelled, "Bitch, you better let her go!"

Before I could even get my hands on a fist full of the girl's hair, I was grabbed by Tyson. "Oh no you don't!" He grabbed me by the waist and hoisted me in the air.

I kept yelling for him to put me down. I watched in the air as Talia and the tight dress girl did fist windmills. The fight was quickly broken up by two men in the parking lot at the church. Tyson put me down when they separated the two. I ran over to Talia, and he ran over to the girl. I quickly asked if she was okay.

She said, "Let's just get out of here."

I was so embarrassed as I got in the car as all the saints looked at us like we were heathens. Out of all the shenanigans I had done or been a part of, I must say this made the top 10 list as one of the most embarrassing moments in my life. As we drove home, I asked her, "What the hell was that about?"

"I don't know, but it's over with us. I don't even want the money back."

"Look, I know you make decent money, honey, but you getting that money back," I said. "Where he live at?" I should have left that situation alone, but it was about the principle of the situation. It was $400, not $4.

We arrived right at the same time as Tyson and the tight-dress girl. I pulled my car up and rolled down the window. "Hey, playa!"

"Oh, it's these bitches again," said the girl.

"You should be quiet," I said as I put my finger over my lips. "This isn't even about you, sweetie. What you got on that $400 bucks Talia gave you?" I asked Tyson.

He started walking aggressively to the car. "Who the fuck you think you are rolling up to my house like you some gangsta?"

"I'm going to stop you right there, playa." I pointed my mace out the window. "No need to get all aggressive with me, playa, cuz I have no problem using this."

"She ain't getting that money. It's gone; I spent it."

The girl started laughing. "What kind of stupid bitch gives a man money? You ain't getting shit, bitch!"

As much as I wanted to see Talia get her money back it was gone, and he sure as hell wasn't about to get on no payment plan to pay her back. She would just have to chalk it up as a loss.

Fast forward to 2003 while coming out of Cal Bowl in Long Beach one Saturday night. Guess who we ran into? Tyson. I looked at him out the side of my eye as he greeted us.

He said, "Hey Kennedee. You look like you wanna mace me."

Jokingly, I said, "Not tonight, Tyson."

Talia was standing there talking to him like she forgot he owed her $400 and was a cheater, but I didn't. So when they exchanged numbers, I was astounded. However, once she married him the very next year in 2004, I was in total dismay.

The marriage was all good until after she had their first baby in 2005. That's when she realized she had hooked up with a narcissist who had used his charm to woo her over. He used several different methods of coercion in order to obtain control over her. He would shift blame, criticize, manipulate, and dominate her. He would always tell her he was so in love with her, but then turn around to find ways to belittle her, like calling her fat when she was only 5'4" and 125 pounds. It seemed like she couldn't do anything right in his eyes. He would complain about her even hanging his pants wrong on the hanger. Even with all that kind of craziness, Talia tried to keep her household together, but she still had the urge to hang out. There was just one problem with that. Her life had literally changed overnight. She had become a wife and a mother all in the same breath.

With that said, we started seeing less and less of her. Phone conversations became annoying. Either she was putting me on hold every other five minutes to tell li'l Ty, "Stop", "Don't", "Be quiet", or "Sit down". If she wasn't doing that, you heard Tyson yelling for her to get off the phone to get dinner made or spend more time with him. In addition, she only called me when she had a problem. She only talked when she needed to vent. She was constantly sucking me dry with her issues, running up my daytime minutes on the cell phone, and basically she was just using me to her benefit. She started making me feel like I should be paid to be her therapist. We all go through peaks and valleys in our lives. Talia and I had been friends for a long time. Her "user friendly" ways had intensified since she got married. She was wearing down the friendship and things just weren't very balanced anymore.

On top of that, Tyson never really liked me after the church parking lot brawl. He insisted that I had egged her on to do that. Hmm, I wonder where he got that idea from? He thought I was a bad influence on her or a detriment to their marriage. That was a whole other problem within itself. I tried distancing myself from Talia so her marriage could have a chance without unnecessary problems, but Talia didn't care. She still wanted to hang out and be friends. Tyson not liking me made the friendship difficult. I didn't want to cause problems in her marriage, but since it wasn't a problem for

Talia, I tried not to worry about it too much. Emil and I were still living the semi-single wild and free life.

Talia wanted to still hang out with the crew like old times, but Tyson was not having it. Tyson was cool, but he just thought married folks didn't have no business up in no clubs or club-like atmospheres. He had no problem letting her go to brunch, lunch, dinner, spa, movies, etc. But the club? He wasn't having it. I had been over the club scene by my late 20's. I honestly did not see the appeal in it. To an extent, I'd have to agree with Tyson. It's not cool to have aggressive men chasing behind you, sliding and trying to grind you on the dance floor, or hearing the sorry played-out line of "Excuse me, Miss..."

Talia would call and ask us to pick her up to go to the club. However, once we arrived at the house, there was always drama with Tyson. The first attempt to go out ceased when Talia went to go get dressed. She walked into her closet and found only the right half of her pairs of shoes. All the left shoes were missing. This nut had taken all of her left shoes and hid them. She was furious because she couldn't find them anywhere. She called him asking what he did with her shoes. He told her he took them for a ride, and hung up. When she called me to cancel and told me the reason why, I couldn't help but to burst out laughing. It was hilarious! She didn't find humor in the situation at all. But I couldn't help but to laugh hysterically until she finally said, "Kennedee, it's really not that funny."

I said, "Oh hell yes it is!" I jokingly added, "Girl, you better get two black shoes and let's go." But poor Talia didn't find the humor in the joke.

For the next attempt for us to get our boogie on, Talia went to get her hair done to go with us to the club. She had gotten all dressed only to walk out of the bathroom and have Tyson pour water all over her hair. When I got there to pick her up, she opened the doors in tears. She was so hurt that Tyson had gone to such great lengths to stop her from going out. However, I couldn't stop laughing when I saw her. Three hours of sitting in the hair salon just went down the drain along with $60. He knew that for sure she wasn't going nowhere with no jacked-up do. She refused to go even though I told her not to let one monkey stop the show and to just slap some mousse or gel on her hair and roll out anyway. Shoot, if it had been me, I would've slapped some gel in my hair, whipped it into a bun, and kept it pushing just to piss him off more. I do have to admit Tyson's tactics were a bit clever and funny as hell.

8

You Ain't Going Nowhere

In Talia's final attempt for a night out, she called
and said Tyson had cleared her to go for the night. I
said, "Are you sure? Because it's always drama or
some type of dilemma."

She said, "Kennedee, I assure you that it will be no
problem this time around."

I picked her up by myself because by this time, the
other girls had grown frustrated with her not being
able to go due to Tyson's antics. When I arrived to
pick her up, before I could even get up the stairs to
her apartment, I could hear yelling. Tyson was
telling her how she needed to stay at home and stop

trying to run the streets like she was single and

how she needed to find some married friends to

hang out with instead of trying to still kick it with

us. I could hear her yelling, but couldn't make out

what she was saying. I was tired of standing

outside eavesdropping, trying to determine if I

should ring the bell or leave without her. I finally

decided to ring the bell.

I was amazed when she opened the door to find her

dressed, no wet hair, and matching shoes. I asked,

"So you ready to go?"

She said, "Let me just grab my purse off the

counter." When she turned to get the purse, it was

gone. She said, "I thought it was right here. Let me

check the bedroom." She walked in the bedroom

and came out with her purse with Tyson right behind her holding li'l Ty.

He asked, "So you just going to go out and leave your family behind?"

"You act like I'm leaving forever. I'll be back later, damn!"

He said, "Fine, then I'm taking li'l Ty to my mama's house and going out with my boys."

"Fine!" she shot back. She closed the door and we headed to the car.

On the way to the club, she stated how glad she was to finally be able to get out of the house. As we pulled up, I could see Sage waiting for us. Sage said, "I see the warden finally let you out."

We all laughed, but unfortunately there was truth to it. Tyson acted like more of a warden than a husband. As we approached the line to get in, we heard the bouncer say, "Get your I.D.'s out."

We all started rummaging through our purses to pull out our I.D.'s. All of a sudden I heard Talia say, "Oh no!"

I asked, "What's wrong?"

She said, "I don't have my I.D."

Sage said, "Oh Lord!"

I got to the front of the line and tried to explain to the bouncer that two of the three of us had our identification, and could I give him this whole $20 to let the other slide. He kindly opened up the red velvet rope to let us OUT of line.

Sage said, "Why can't we go in just because she doesn't have her I.D.?"

"It wouldn't be right for us to go in without her."

Sage said, "She can just go sit in the car."

Talia frowned. "What I look like sitting in the car while y'all in there having a good time? You guys aren't being fair."

Sage said, "Fair? Please! You're the one no one hears from until you want or need something or want to talk about that crazy-ass husband of yours. We hardly even see you anymore. It's not our fault that you chose this life. You're married; we're not. You can't expect us to be at your beck and call whenever you're ready. We have only turned into your 'social friends'. We never hear from you, and when we do, it's because you want to hang out or vent. Maybe you should find some other friends to use."

Yikes! Sage had just said a mouthful, but to be honest, she wasn't saying anything that we all hadn't said about Talia since she had gotten married. I had to interrupt and say, "Look, let's not have this li'l pow wow in the parking lot. Either you're going in or you're not, it's that simple." She turned to get back in line as Talia and I made our way back to the car.

As I pulled up to Talia's apartment complex, she apologized for ruining my evening. I said, "Don't worry about it."

"I can't believe Sage said that about me!"

"Well, to be honest, it's kind of true."

"How so, Kennedee?" she asked.

"You haven't noticed that you only call one of us when you're attempting to get away from here?" I said as I pointed to the apartment.

"You know, you all are really tripping! I just think that you guys are jealous that I'm married and you guys aren't."

"Are you serious right now?" I asked disbelievingly. "If being married consists of this, then you, my dear, you can have it."

"What's that supposed to mean?" she asked.

"It means you can't have the single life while being married."

She got upset, said a quick good night, and slammed the door. I yelled, "Hey!" out the window.

When she turned around to see what I wanted, I said, "Don't call me just to hang out sometimes. Call to check on a sistah." Then I winked at her, and she nodded okay. "Oh, by the way, you better go pick up li'l Ty from his granny's house since you back so early."

"I could use some me time, so he can stay there 'til his Dad picks him after hanging with the fellas."

"Alrighty." As I watched her go up the steps, I could tell she was in total denial about her decision to marry Tyson. For the sake of the friendship that night, we'd agree to disagree for now.

Before I could even get home my phone was ringing. I looked at it and saw a number that I didn't recognize, so I didn't answer. The phone rang a few times with the same number. I picked up the phone to hear Talia crying hysterically. She said she was around the corner from the house at the 7-11 and she wanted to know if I could come get her.

"Of course! I will be right there."

As I pulled up I saw Talia pacing in front of the store. When she saw my car, she raced over and hopped in. She said, "Oh my goodness, you won't believe what happened! When I walked in the house, it was pitch dark. When I went to turn the lights on, that fool was sitting in the dark in the corner. He asked if I had a good time out. I told him I wasn't in the mood to talk about it. He immediately started fussing at me for going out. I told him to calm down and let's just talk about this tomorrow when he had a cooler head. I went into the bedroom to go to bed. He came in the room, ripped the covers off of me, pulled me by the leg,

put me over his head, carried me out the front door,

and put me out the apartment. I banged on the

door, begging him to let me back in. He finally

opened the door and shoved my purse out the crack

of the door. He told me since I wanted to go out so

bad, I could stay out there. There is no way in hell

I'm staying there tonight!"

I thought to myself, *Sounds like you didn't have a choice.*
Aloud, I said, "Well, you know that you can stay at

my house."

"Cool, and I'll just go home tomorrow morning."

"Yeah, we can just go get your stuff in the morning."

"My stuff?"

"Yeah, your stuff, so you can get away from his crazy ass."

"That's my husband; I'm not leaving him."

I just kind of gave her a blank stare because I didn't know what else to say next.

The following morning when I took her back to the apartment, I walked upstairs with her. I had my mace in my hand just in case he was still feeling crazy. As we walked in the door, he was at the kitchen counter. He came and kissed her on the cheek and said, "Where you been, babe?" He acted like nothing had happened. "I got some eggs and bacon for you if you're hungry, babe. Hey Kennedee. I see you got your handy mace out as usual."

I retorted, "Well, ya never know when someone needs a taste of mace! It's never too early for craziness."

"You want a plate?" Talia asked as she made her way into the kitchen.

I stood at the door dazed and confused. I felt like I was in a bad episode of the Twilight Zone. Both of them were acting like a big fight hadn't just transpired twelve hours ago. I said, "No, I'm good. Are you good, Talia?"

She said, "I'm fine."

"Well, I guess I'll go."

"Okay, talk to you soon."

As I turned to walk out the door, Tyson said, "It's good to see you, Kennedee. You know ya'll like thirty years old trying to be up in the club, and that is not a good look for you. Have a good one."

I turned and said, "Uh, okay." I thought to myself, What the fuck? I guess he didn't get the memo. I do what I want to do. Him telling me I was too old to be in the club didn't make me blink. It was one thing to tell yo' wife what to do, but he sure in hell wasn't running me! As I walked down the stairs, I took a long sigh and thanked God I wasn't in her shoes.

9

Love the Way You Lie

Sage was still working at the county for DPSS. She was the second of the group to get married. I wasn't surprised when she got married in 2008. After all, she and Logan had been together for a long time. He was well-established, had good credit, was handsome, had no offspring running around, and he had his own place. You could tell he was a pushover when it came to Sage. There wasn't nothing he wouldn't do for her. Anything she'd ask for, it was hers. He really loved her.

Sage had a very strong personality with lots of confidence. You couldn't tell her she wasn't fine.

Even though she was a size 16, in her mind, she walked around like she was a size 6. It made her more lovable because she didn't care what other

 people thought of her. Logan...well, he was real laidback. He wasn't too much of a talker. He would be satisfied spending the weekend at home in front of the TV. Sage liked to be out and be seen and to have a good time. She would say, "Girl, I look too good to be sitting at home."

Unlike Talia, my friendship with Sage didn't change much once she got married. However, I noticed a change in Sage. She had been a social drinker over the years, but she started becoming a binge drinker, and on top of that she was smoking weed and hanging out like she was twenty-one all over again. I didn't have time for that. I was thirty-three and trying to move forward in life to be successful. So once she started doing all that, I had to distance myself from her. Our circle never dabbled in drugs. We may have tossed back a few drinks every now and again, but nothing too hardcore.

When Sage started cheating on Logan shortly after being married, the friendship turned sour. She wanted to use me as her alibi when she would sneak away with her men. She would call me giggling and laughing while I heard a guy's voice in the background, and she would say, "Hey, do me a favor. If Logan calls, you, just tell him I'm with you." Or she would say, "Don't call the house because I'm supposed to be with you."

I finally had to ask why she was doing him like that. She responded, "He's too nice, and he gets on my nerves with all that."

So I guess she wanted a narcissistic fool like Tyson. I don't know. Most guys aren't looking to get married. They're content with coming over to watch your cable and run up your electric bill and put a dent in your couch. Back then and even now it's hard to get men to commit, but she had a man that was truly committed in a marriage. It baffled me as to why she would do anything to jeopardize that.

I played the alibi game a few times, but I finally had to put my foot down and tell her no. Everybody knows I don't condone cheating, so I don't know why the hell she would think I would be okay for covering for her. I'm not lying for nobody. You're man/woman enough to cheat, be man/woman enough to deal with the consequences. I'd been used as an alibi long enough that I was no longer going to be a willing participant and knowingly provide an alibi for her again (I say KNOWINGLY because sometimes people don't even know when they're being used as one). I don't want to be involved with that shit, flat out.

Logan was no longer as easygoing and laidback as he was when they first got married. He had mustered up some balls of courage out of nowhere. He was tired of being the pushover and being taken advantage of. The more he tried to put his foot down, the more she cheated. He'd tell her, "You better not be cheating on me, because if I find out, your ass is grass."

Sage would laugh it off and continue to do her thang. It was too li'l too late. It was like trying to make a comeback in the fourth quarter when you thirty points behind with five minutes left in the game. You can't decide to be the MVP of the game once your opponent has taken control, and that's what was happening with her and him.

One day I called her cell phone and she didn't answer, so I tried calling again. To my surprise, Logan picked up the phone. He said, "Hey Kennedee."

I said, "What's up, Logan?"

"Nothing much."

"Um, can I speak with Sage?"

"Sage left her phone here. I thought she was with you?"

Aw hell! I wasn't a quick thinker when it came to lying for someone else, so this totally caught me off-guard. I sighed as I thought of what lie I could tell to cover for her or try to figure out what to say to cover for her. As I was thinking, my thoughts were interrupted by Logan.

"Um...hello?" I heard his fingers snap through the phone. "I know you heard what I asked."

"Um, hello, I was thinking."

"Who told you to think? It's not a hard question. You're a smart girl. Either you've seen my wife or you haven't. It's just that simple."

Whoo! Did he just say who told me to think? Wow! In the back of my mind, I was like, Is this clown really trying to check me? I yelled, "Before you call yourself checking anybody else, check yourself, check yourself again, and then check yourself one more time. You don't ever try to check me like I'm your bitch. Don't get fucking smart with me. I don't know, maybe she laid up with the next man since you over there snapping your fingers like a li'l bitch."

He gasped and said, "Fuck you, cunt!" and hung up the phone.

I know that wasn't very nice on my part. Man, I had drama in my own relationships, and I sure in hell didn't need to be involved in anyone else's. Plus, I didn't know what to tell that man. Clearly this is

why I told her to stop using me for an alibi. I tried
my best to stay out of other folks' relationships, but
somehow I knew I would end up the culprit.

Without a shadow of a doubt, I knew she was in
trouble, and I had no way of letting her know since
she didn't have her phone. I was on the fence about
what to do and how Logan might approach her. I
thought I'd head Sage off at the corner of her house
before she got home. I hopped in the car and headed
to her house. What I thought would take a few
minutes turned into a few hours. I was out there
from 9:00 p.m. until about 1-something in the
morning when I finally saw her car hit the corner I
hurried up and started my ignition and begin to
flash the high beams. As I drove up to her car, she
stopped in the middle of the street. I pulled up on

the side of her and motioned for her to roll down the window.

As she rolled down the window, I said, "I called your cell, but Logan answered."

She said, "Yeah, I keep a second phone." She raised a phone up in the air.

"What's that? I thought you left your phone."

"I did, but I keep a Boost phone so my boo's can call me on this phone."

"Are you serious?" I asked incredulously.

"Hell yeah!"

"He thought you were with me."

"Well, that's what I told him."

"Why would you do that? I really don't want to be mixed up in this mess. Look, don't be mad at me for what I'm about to tell you."

"What did you say?" Sage asked.

"Nothing, but when he got smart with me, I kinda sort of blurted out that you was probably laid up with the next man."

"Why would you say that?" Sage exploded.

"It kinda just came out, plus I didn't want to be involved in your mess."

She started rolling up the window as I was still talking and began to drive off. I followed her as she pulled up to her driveway. As she got out of the car, I yelled, "Sage, it wasn't done intentionally. I'm really sorry."

"Yeah, you sorry, alright - a sorry-ass friend who can't even be there when they are needed."

"Needed for what? To lie? I told you, don't use me no more to cover for you, yet you did, then you just want me to pull something out my ass to cover for you. Oh no, darling, you ain't going to flip your deception on me."

"You always talking about loyalty, Kennedee. Where's the loyalty now?"

"This don't have nothing to do with loyalty. This is about you getting me caught up in the mix. I can't with you right now." I got back in the car and pulled off.

I went back and forth for days debating if I was wrong, and in some way I was. I let my anger get the best of me and I lashed out with harsh words.

But on the other hand, she had involved me unknowingly in her deception, and I was totally caught off-guard.

I waited for about a week to call her to own up to my wrongs and make 'em right, because sometimes you can be right, and still be wrong. When I finally did, she sent me to voicemail a few times. Finally I gave up on trying to rectify the situation. A few minutes later, I heard my phone chime. When I picked it up, I saw it was a picture message from her. When I opened it up, I saw boxes with clothes, shoes, and purses flowing out of them with a note on top that read "Get the fuck out, tramp." The picture message was followed with a text that read, "This is entirely your fault."

Pump the brakes. My fault? Wow! She couldn't see the forest for the trees. I was floored, and I was done. I wouldn't take the blame for breaking an already-broken marriage. I knew she would eventually get over it.

By this time, Facebook had become the new "it" thing to do. She and I were still on each other's friends list even after the incident. I had never been big on Facebook. I would just pop in and out, hit "like" or comment on something every now and then and keep it pushing. But on one particular day when I logged in, I noticed her all up and down my newsfeed. She had posted the picture she had sent to me, saying, "Folks just don't want to see other folks happy."

So I kinda just said to myself, Hmm... That was on her if she wanted to put her business in the streets like that. Then I saw her post, "Bitches can't keep a man so they always trying to break up what you got." Next I saw, "Bitches stay up in the abortion clinic."

Ouch! That hurt. I knew she was talking about me. It was no secret that I had a few trips to the abortion clinic. I wasn't proud of it, but I sure didn't want everybody and they mama on Facebook to know it. Then I saw someone's comment: "Damn, Sage, you going in on somebody today. Who is it? Drop a name." I knew she liked to tell other people's business still as an adult, so my heart began to race. *She better not do it or that's her ass.*

I know you're probably thinking, well, didn't you write a whole book about your past? I sho' did. But it's one thing for me to air my dirty laundry; you sure in the hell can't! I waited and kept hitting refresh on the computer every few seconds to see if she was going to respond. Finally I saw a comment from her and it said, "Nah, I ain't going to say, because unlike other bitches, I don't put other people's business out there like that."

She couldn't be serious now! Ain't that the pot calling the kettle black? The nerve!

So I picked up the phone and called. Yet again, I was sent to voicemail. It was apparent she called herself not talking to me. So I hit her with a text. I said, "You real funny, bitch. Don't make statuses on Facebook to disrespect me, blatantly or indirectly.

Don't make me forget we were once friends and come knocking at your door. Don't play with me. You already know my get-down. You don't want it with me." I hit send and off went my terroristic threats. I say terrorist threats because when the police arrived at my door this is what she had called them about.

Yep, the heffa called the police on me. I was in pure shock as I stood at my doorstep for forty-five minutes trying to explain to the police there was no seriousness to the text that I sent, that it was a small disagreement that had been diffused. Well, there was some truth to the text, but I didn't feel like going to jail that night or any other night for that matter. Been there, done that.

When they left, I rushed to the phone to call her not to try to be her friend again, but why the hell would she call the police on me when it wasn't even that serious? Instead of her picking up, I heard the automated system saying, "The subscriber you are trying to reach is no longer in service." So I hung up and went to the computer and went to her page. How ironic; I had been deleted. That was cool by me.

You would think that Sage would want a friend who wasn't afraid to get real with her and call her on her shit when necessary. I still struggle with how our friendship ended. Talia asked me if Sage called, would I be friends with her again? I should have been more careful with how much information I shared with her. I trusted her, never thought she would attempt to hurt me with my own secrets so viciously. I felt so betrayed. To answer Talia's

question no. Once the loyalty is gone, I'm cutting

you off period. There's no coming back from that,

no making it right, no tryna fix it. All of a sudden

my stable friendship with Sage had become topsy-

turvy and I found myself determining that she was

no longer a person that I still wanted to call friend.

Sage had become my "frenemy." Please note my

definition of a "frenemy" is someone who used to be

my friend until some unforgivable drama ensued,

and because of it, I don't like you or fuck with you

anymore. They say keep your friends close, and your

enemies closer. But I'm not one to keep my enemies

close to me.

In essence, friends don't turn into enemies; they just

show you that they never were your friends to

begin with. Talia and I were in her circle of friends, however, her actions made her become an "enemy" to both of us. Talia didn't want to retain the friendship with her either. She couldn't be trusted. Would she decide to air out Talia's business next when she got upset again? I didn't have to ask for Talia to sever ties with her because even she had enough of her telling all of our business over the years. There just ain't no middle ground-you're either "for" me...or "against" me. Clearly she had chosen to be against me the moment she attempted to air out my business on social media. Remember, a real enemy can never be a friend...and a real friend can never be an enemy.

10

Differences

By 2009, five years into her marriage, Talia started
to notice a sudden increase in Tyson's online
activity. He was on his laptop all the time and she
knew it wasn't work-related. He suddenly became
very active on social networking sites, and he
wasn't just chatting it up with old friends. He was
making some new ones too, and I'm not talking
about no guys. He was on there liking all the half-
nude pics, the kind with boobies sticking out. He
even had a new e-mail account that Talia didn't
have the password to. Tip of the iceberg: whenever
she would walk in the room, he would close chat

windows or the laptop screen itself and become uncomfortable all of a sudden.

"Is he trying to hide his communication with someone?" she asked.

"Uh, hell yeah!" I said. "I see curiosity is about to get the best of you. Try to look up his history to see if you can find something, and if it has been erased, you know he definitely has something to hide." Why did I suggest that? That opened a can of worms that I wished I had never opened.

It's funny when men think they can lie to you and get away with it that easily. Men obviously aren't aware of our ridiculously strong radar that can smell a lie a mile away. Now we all indulge in little white lies every now and then. But if you notice that your husband has been lying to you way too often, if he hasn't been looking you in the eye when asked where he was or why he's late and if he has one too many excuse for his actions, confront his ass.

Turns out Talia didn't have to do anything. Tyson had just upgraded from his Blackberry to an iPhone, however, he still had the Blackberry laying around. Talia decided to plug it up and see if she could find anything in his old call log. As she scrolled through the call log, she saw numerous calls from someone named Cherie. When she looked in the text messages, she saw messages from Cherie as well. The messages kept going back and forth with Cherie saying how much she missed Tyson and how much she wanted to see him. She was asking when she could see him, he was calling her babe and she was calling him honey. My heart ached as my friend told me what she found in the phone. I knew how badly Talia wanted her marriage to work, so to find out that Tyson was cheating on her was devastating.

Talia had written down Cherie's number to call her. She invited me over and told me she was going to call Cherie.

"For what?" I asked.

"To see what's going on," she said.

"How about you wait and ask Tyson what's going on?" Then I paused and said, "But he may deny and lie about everything even though you have all of this evidence. You know how men are. You catch them in the bed with another woman, and they be like, 'Why you tripping? This my sister.' And you just look with a blank stare like how stupid do you think I am?"

"You ain't never lied. So what you think I should do?"

"I think that my name is Bennett and I ain't in it. Girl, I get tired of trying to help y'all out with your relationship problems and don't nobody listen. You do the total opposite of what I say. So you'll have to figure this out on your own, darling. Just don't sell your soul tryin' to buy that dream."

With that being said, she picked up her cell phone and commenced to dialing. "Hello, can I speak to Cherie" This is Talia, Tyson's wife." There was a silence then I saw Talia put down the phone.

"What happened?" I asked.

"She said don't call her asking questions about my husband and to ask him."

"I hate to tell you, but, well, I told you so. Whatever is going on, you know she's going to tell Tyson you just called her. Be prepared for him to confront you about this."

"So! I don't care; I hope she does."

I had been through so much in relationships that I could almost foretell what was going to happen before it happened. I wasn't surprised when she called me and said that when Tyson got home, he was furious. He told her that whatever happened between them should stay between them and that she should not be contacting third parties with questions.

I guess that wasn't good enough for Talia, because the next day, she texted me asking me to come by before 7:00. I thought it was strange, but I passed through there on my way from work. I knocked on the door and she greeted me with yoga pants and a sweatshirt. I said, "You getting ready to work out?"

"No, girl, come on in. I got something to show you."

As I made my way to the dining room table, I said, "What's up? What's the urgency?"

She sat down in the chair next to me to show me her phone. "Let me tell you. I went on his friends list on Facebook to see if he had a Cherie for a friend. I came across this chick right here."

"She looks familiar," I said. "Do we know her or something?"

"Yeah, we know her."

"Okay, from where?" I asked.

"You don't remember? Look closer."

I looked closer, but a name didn't click. "I don't know just tell me."

"It's the girrrrrl."

"What girl?" I asked.

She huffed, "The girl from the church I had the fight with that time."

"Oh my God!" I yelled. "I can't believe this!"

"Me neither."

I clicked on her pictures.

"And why is she married with three kids?"

"Married?" I asked, shocked. "Man, she is a greedy bitch! She got a man and trying to take yours too. That's so trifling!"

"Yep, that's why I told her if she didn't stop contacting Tyson, I was going to let her husband know."

"Oh no you didn't!"

"Oh yes I did!"

"What she say?"

"That she got my man and her man handled. She run this."

"I know she didn't go there, girl!" I'm not one usually at a loss for words, but I was just stunned how bold this chick was. The writing was on the wall; it couldn't be any clearer. She needed to leave Tyson's unfaithful ass alone. However, I didn't say that because she needed to make that decision for herself.

She said, "I need a drink and a taco. Let's go to El Torito for Taco Tuesday in Lakewood. Please," she begged. "I just need to get out the house."

"Where's li'l Ty?"

"He's at my parent's house, so we can hang out for a li'l while."

"Cool, I'm with it, let's roll."

"I'll drive, she offered.

"What? You never wanna drive."

"I know you probably don't wanna drive after driving all the way from downtown LA."

"I sure don't, I agreed."

So we hopped in her car. When the exit came to get off on Lakewood, she kept driving. I said, "You know you missed the exit, right?" She acted like she didn't hear me, so I repeated myself.

"I know," she said.

"Well, are we going somewhere different or did you change the location?"

"We are going to Cherie's house. I did a people search and found her address."

"Wait! Please tell me we are not about to go over this chick's house causing havoc!"

"Yep, we sure are, so hold on to your seat, KD."

"Talia, you should've told me this before I got in the car with you. We are not twenty years old anymore, we are thirty-four. We too old for some mess like this. "C'mon, don't be stupid. You're not thinking."

"Be quiet!" she snapped. "I'm not trying to hear all that shit right now."

I was in flames at how she pulled me into this drama. I should've known something was up when she wanted to drive. I sat there quietly as she drove up to a cream and beige house.

"C'mon," she said as she opened her door to get out.

"Oh no, honey, I will be a spectator from this passenger chair."

"Alright!"

I watched as she made her way to the door to ring the bell. I couldn't hear too much of anything. I just saw Talia using her hands while she was talking. The conversation escalated when I heard someone say, "Bitch, you don't know me! I will fuck you up!"

As Talia started to step down from the porch, I saw the screen door fly open. "Bitch, you better get off my porch!" Cherie ran out.

Talia was almost at the end of the driveway when she turned and said, "If you see a bitch, come whip a bitch's ass!"

I sighed. I knew things were about to get uglier than what they already were, so I made my way out of the car. Before I could get to the driveway, Cherie marched up to Talia and didn't say a word. She just took her left hand, grabbed her by the hair, and punched her in the cheek. I hurried up and ran to the driveway to pull them apart. I was using all my strength to break them apart, but they both had each other by the hair.

I screamed, "Let her go!"

"You tell her to let me go!" yelled Cherie.

"No, you let her go and she will let you go," I said. She wouldn't budge, so I did what any good friend would do. I got back in the car. Just kidding! I reached up under the two and hit the girl in the abdomen. She immediately let Talia go as she doubled over holding her abdomen. She started yelling, calling us crazy bitches as she fell to the ground.

"I'm calling the police on you!"

I picked up Talia's glasses and grabbed her by the arm. "Let's get the hell out of here."

When we got in the car, I handed over her glasses. I looked over at her. She had her hair all over her head, looking like Don King. I could tell she was hurt, but all she had was a small bruise on her cheek, and the frame on her glasses was bent. She looked over and said, "Are you okay, KD?"

"Really? Really, Talia? We too old for this shit. We grown. I don't handle things like this anymore. I have a career to think about. I can't be out in these streets fighting. You know if I get a record or an arrest it could jeopardize my job. Why would you put me in harm's way?"

"I'm sorry. I just needed you to go. I didn't want to go by myself."

"I can't even talk to you right now. Just hurry up and get me back to my car."

When we arrived back at the car, I hurried up and got out. As I opened the door to my car, Talia asked, "Can you come in 'til Tyson gets here?"

"No, I can't. That's your drama and you're going to have to deal with it. I gotta go."

"Hold up," she said.

"What do you want now?" I asked.

"Thanks for having my back like you always have."

"That's the problem; I always have your back. When have you ever had mine? I don't recall you being there for me when I went to ride on my lying, cheating, abusive, using men. Where were you? You were always trying to tell me you didn't want to get involved, telling me not to go, that it was not worth it. Remember that? How dare you continuously throw me in your drama? This is not a healthy friendship. It is very one-sided. I'm tired of being there and it not being reciprocated."

"I'm sorry!" she yelled. "I never intended to hurt you; I never intended to use you. I just wanted you to be there for me."

"Well, why don't you try and be there for me once in a while?" I closed the door and drove off.

When I got home, she texted me saying, "Sorry."

I just couldn't deal with her. I needed to give myself a few days to calm down. I had worked so hard in my own personal life to manage my anger by going to counseling, and I had learned to think before I reacted. I felt like her actions had caused me to take two steps back instead of two steps forward. I had to reassess if I really needed to keep someone like her in my life. She had been cool to be around while we were growing up, but in adulthood, she had changed a bit too much for my taste. All the using, calling when she needed something, and using me to dump all her drama on me had become exhausting. She had become more of a liability than an asset to the friendship.

I didn't talk with her for three weeks. When I finally answered her call one afternoon, she told me that she was filing for divorce from Tyson. She had finally had enough. I was happy for her that she was finally getting out of her tumultuous marriage. The moment of happiness lasted for only a hot second as she fixed her lips to ask me to serve Tyson with the divorce papers. I don't know what part of Crazyland she was living in, but after watching *All Worked Up* on truTV, you couldn't pay me to serve nobody. Those people getting served on that show would go into rages like the server was the responsible party for causing the situation. No way, Jose! I wasn't doing this for her. Plus I knew Tyson was low-key cray-cray. I kindly told her that if she paid a fee, the sheriff's department would serve him the papers.

She was furious that I wouldn't comply with her request. "You can't do this one favor for me, KD?"

"No ma'am, I can't, and I won't. This is where I have to draw the line. I can't allow you to keep putting me in the line of fire."

"Fine, then we're not friends anymore."

"Is that you what you want? You'll be stuck with Emil's ass, just you and Emil."

"I guess she'll be the last one standing then," she said.

"You can't coerce me into doing anything that I don't want to do or give me no ultimatums. You don't wanna be my friend? Hold on for a second while I try to give a care. Not! Girl, please knock it off. At this point, I could give two shits if you rock with me or not. See, there's a big difference between rolling solo because ain't nobody fucking with you no more or because you can roll all by yourself. I rolls by myself because I choose to. Losing one more friend ain't going to make or break me. Bye."

Just like that, twenty-one years of friendship ended. Whew! It felt like a burden had been lifted off my shoulders immediately. I'm a team player, but once I had enough of you operating on a selfish, self-centered, all-about-me type of attitude....I'm done looking out for you.

11

Two Sides to Every Story

Back in the early 2000's, I decided I needed a li'l more Jesus in my life. I began attending church on a regular basis again. Every time the church doors were open, I was there. Bible study, Sunday morning service, Sunday evening service, you name it, I was there. I was happy that I was getting more involved in the church because I had been raised in the church. But through my adult years, my attendance wasn't as stellar as it was when I was going with my parents.

I was really into this church and then Jayden arrived. Jayden was the new minister of music. He was 6'6" with the prettiest caramel-brown eyes, and you could tell he was a slave to the gym

because his body was banging. Jayden was very

talented. He could play that organ, and boy, could

he sing! He had some pipes on him. He caught my

eye the first Sunday he started playing. After

church, I made sure to give him a good ole church

handshake.

"Hi, I'm Kennedee."

"I'm Jayden. Have you been coming here long?"

"For a few months now."

He asked if I would like to go out sometime. I said

sure and gave him my number. I knew dating him

would be a breath of fresh air compared to what I

had been through in my other relationships. Jayden

was something else. He was like a Christian bad

boy. There was no doubt in my mind that Jayden loved Jesus by all the Scriptures he quoted. He had a tricked-out Escalade with the Not of this World decal on his back window, and his multiple CD player consisted of only the latest contemporary gospel tunes. He even had a cross on his right bicep, and to top it off, his mom was an evangelist and his dad was a preacher. I had finally found the package, a real church boy that could do no wrong. Ha! People tend to insinuate that because a man is in the church they are without flaws, but sometimes those are the guys who need Jesus the most.

I had Emil pick me up from Jayden's house one afternoon because Emil and I were heading out to the spa. When she arrived, I told her let me go upstairs real quick to grab my stuff. "I will be right back." I couldn't find what I was looking for so it was taking longer than I expected.

All of a sudden I heard Emil yell, "KD!"

I quickly stopped what I was doing to rush to see what she wanted. When I arrived at the base of the stairs, I stood there in shock as I saw Jayden jump up, zipping up his pants. Jayden began to say, "I can explain."

I just stood there shaking my head. "I don't want to hear it."

Jayden grabbed my arm tightly and said, "Where do you think you're going?"

"You're hurting me! You better let me go!"

He quickly apologized for grabbing my arm. "I'm sorry, don't leave. Don't you want to even hear what I have to say?"

"I've seen enough; I'm leaving," I said in disgust.

Please, babe, let me explain."

"Fine. I've heard it all, but maybe you've got something new to say."

"Emil is the one who came over to the couch. She said, 'Let me see how big your dick is'."

Emil interrupted, saying, "You're lying!"

"Wait a minute, Emil, let him finish. Go ahead and finish, Jayden."

"I told her no and she bent over and started to zip down my pants. That's when she called you downstairs. Honest, babe, I wouldn't lie; I'm a Christian."

"Ha! Like that ever stopped anyone from telling a li'l white lie," I scoffed.

Emil said, "That's not true. As soon as you went upstairs, he said, 'Hey Emil', and when I looked over to see what he wanted, he pulled his dick out his pants and shook it at me. Who are you going to believe, me or him? I've known you for almost your whole life, Kennedee. You know I wouldn't do you like that.

My face frowned up with disgust at this whole situation. I wasn't sure what happened while I was up those stairs. All I knew for sure was that one of them was lying. I've had my fair share of liars and cheaters. As much as I tried not to presume everyone was like the next man, this situation sure wasn't helping. After all, I hoped Emil would know better to try and pull a stunt like that on me. Sooooooo....I had to make a quick decision without thinking it over. I turned and said, "I don't do liars. I'm out, Jayden. God speed be with you." Trust is the glue that holds relationships together. I had only known Jayden for a hot second, and I had known Emil since we were kids.

Charge it to the Game

Over the years we had all become successful in our own ways. Emil was now a makeup artist for Hollywood stars. She was in charge of the makeup department on major television and movie sets. She had always loved to beat her face in makeup, and was really good at what she did so I wasn't surprised at her success. I was happy for her to be doing well, because that's what real friends do: they push and challenge each other. I always challenged and encouraged all the ladies to dream, plan, and work harder. After all, real friends should motivate each other.

But then I noticed she was becoming more competitive. I had to raise an eyebrow. A little healthy competition can be good in a friendship as long as you're motivating each other for more in life. However, it wasn't that type of competition. When we would be out for drinks at a lounge or the club and a guy would try and talk to me, she would run interference. She would interrupt if she saw a guy talking to me by saying, "Hey there, I am her friend Emil. How are you?" Then she'd start batting them damn fake eyelashes.

I would roll my eyes because clearly she was trying to steal the spotlight off me. I wasn't tripping. In my mind I was my only competition. She wasn't a threat to me because as hard as she tried, even on her best day, she couldn't compete with me when it came to the men. She had definitely changed for the worse over the years. She had grown into a more curvaceous shape, which made her even more conceited. But on top of that, she had gotten an "I think I'm better than you" type of attitude that always made me want to slap the shit out of her even though she was my friend.

I've always been the serial dater of the group. I loved the fellas, and the fellas loved me. After you became my ex, I was on to the next. However, when I met Bailey back in like 2000, I think. There was something different. Don't get me wrong, he was fine. He reminded me of Steve Urkel when he turned into Stefon. He had the prettiest smile with dimples and the nicest white teeth. The only problem was hanging with him was like hanging with one of the girls. He never wanted to get physical; all he wanted to do was shop and eat.

Now I find nothing wrong with a metrosexual man. And if you don't know what a metrosexual man is, that's the type of man that is meticulous about his grooming and appearance, like getting a manicure, pedicure, haircuts on a regular, nice wardrobe, etc.

Bailey liked doing all the things of a metrosexual, however, when I noticed he got the HIGH gloss clear polish I had to raise an eyebrow. I was like, damn, his nails were shining more than mine and I had on colored polish. On top of that, he arched his eyebrows. Yes, his eyebrows! I mean, there is nothing wrong with a man cleaning up the bushy hair in between the middle of his eyes to stop the unibrow, but it's another thing to get them shaped up. I drew the line there. He was a straight up divo - not a diva, but a divo. I knew something wasn't on the up and up with him and my instincts are rarely wrong. Don't misunderstand me, I have no problem with the LGBT community, but hey, if you're balling for the other team, at least give me the option to figure out if I want to deal with you or not. 9 times out of 10 I would probably be gone with the wind, but he would have gotten an "A" for honesty if he had been honest. Since he wasn't, I had to roll with my gut. Since I was unsure of his sexuality, I put him in the friend zone. Plus I was interested to see if the myth that gay men make the best girlfriends was true. So we still hung out and did the same stuff, but I knew it wasn't leading to anything.

In 2009, I invited him and Emil along for my company's Christmas party. After the party we went to Glow Lounge inside the Marriott. We got so tipsy that we had to take a cab back to my house. Emil slept in the guest room and Bailey slept on the couch. The next morning when I woke up, I found everyone in their respective places. I began to wake everyone up.

"You ain't got to go home, but ya got to get the hell out of here. So which one of you will be taking me to my car?"

Emil said, "I guess I will."

Bailey said, "I'll roll with y'all."

So we drove back to the Marriott where I'd left my car. Emil asked, "You wanna grab some breakfast at Roscoe's?"

I said, "As yummy as that sounds, I'm tired. I'm going to go home and get some rest."

"I'll roll with you," Bailey said to Emil. "I'm starving."

So off to breakfast the two of them went. I didn't think too much about it because, well, I thought he was gay.

In the weeks to follow, Bailey started hanging out more with Emil. I was a li'l jealous. After all, he was supposed to be my "gay" best friend first. Then everything changed one day while we were eating out at PF Chang's for lunch. He reached over and gave Emil a kiss. I had to close my eyes, shake my head, and reopen my eyes to make sure I wasn't tripping. So to validate that I wasn't seeing things, I said, "Bailey, did you kiss Emil?"

"Yes," he confirmed.

I immediately became infuriated. It's not because I wanted Bailey or anything. Emil had just broken the number one code of the circle. You don't date your friend's ex. This is a sticky subject for some people because some people say it's cool as long as approval is given. Even if you did come to me for approval, all of my exes and all of my friends' exes were off-limits. Point. Blank. Period. Don't ask me again. If I catch ya doing it after I've made it clear, that's your ass. I don't give a damn if we dated forty years ago, he is still off limits. It's just a respect thing for me, which was something Emil was lacking.

I asked, "How long has this been going on?"

Emil said, "It's been a minute...ever since that Christmas party, so for about two months. You cool with it, right?"

"Hell no! You can do anything you want, but like all actions, there are consequences. Dating my ex will change our friendship without a doubt. So, depending on how important of a friend I am to you, this might be something you want to consider. Now what are you going to do? We dated for a few months, and you only dated him for a few weeks."

"What difference does it make? Plus sometimes you can't help the way you feel about a person." Then she leaned over to kiss him.

Well, I guess that was my answer. I said, "Waiter, please, I need my check and a to-go box."

The waiter said, "But you just got your food. Is something wrong with the service or food? Is there something I can do?"

"Unless you have better people for me to dine with, then no. The people at this table have ruined my appetite, that's all."

Emil asked, "So why you mad?"

"Are you serious right now? Look, I brought him around because I thought he was gay and would be a cool friend, not for you to date." Yep! I said it right in front of him, and I didn't feel no shame about it, because my gut was never wrong when it came to men. "The mere fact that y'all doing all that touching and kissing...ugh! Y'all smiling' and shit in my face, acting like I'm supposed to be glad to break bread with you. I am so good. It don't matter

Kennedee Devoe

how long I haven't talked to him, all that should matter is that I have and you should want no parts of him for that reason itself."

The waiter arrived just in time. When he got to the table, I handed him $30. "This should cover my tab." I scraped my food into the box. I sat there with a smirk on my face while sipping the half-finished Mojito in front of me. "You know what? If this drink didn't cost me $10, whoo! Cuz what I really feel like doing is throwing my drink in your caked-up face, Emil, and clearing the whole damn table with my hands." As I got up, still sipping on the last of the drink, as they both looked scared. I stood up, dusted off my dress, and said, "Instead I'm just going to say peace out and y'all enjoy ya lunch without me."

Please keep in my mind this next scenario was a few months into attending counseling for my anger management...tee hee! So then I thought about it. I walked back to the table. I said, "Since you like my leftovers so much, you can enjoy these." I dumped my to-go food dead in Emil's lap. That made me feel a li'l better as I walked away in disgust. I thought for sure he was gay. I don't know, maybe I was wrong. I felt hurt and betrayed; she was my friend. The competitive side of her had been taken to a whole other level.

The next day she called me. "I honestly was not okay with the situation. I'm not sure what part of that don't you understand. I've tolerated all I can from seeing you all together, and bringing him to lunch like that and acting all in love and shit was not cool. So from this day forward, if you're going to date him, fine, but all I ask is that you don't call me anymore because we're not cool."

"What's your problem? You want him back or something?"

"Pleeeeasse, he is gay anyways, so you can have him."

"You weren't saying that before when you were dating. Why all of sudden is he gay? You're just saying that because you're jealous."

"Jealous of what, your girlfriend? Oops, I mean your boyfriend? I can't even believe you right now. If this had been a different ex, you and I wouldn't be having this conversation. I would be beating your ass instead."

"How are you going to come at me like that? I thought we were friends.

I said, "If we were friends, you wouldn't think this was alright. I loved you. You were like my sister, but you traded your soul for dick. Bye, hoe." I wasn't going to be able to get past that incident. I was naïve to believe she wouldn't hurt me this way. This whole scenario made me question her story about Jayden that one day. Had I been too trusting to believe she wouldn't do me that way? Did I really get the full scope of the story that day, or did I just jump to conclusions? No need to dwell on the past because I had made my decision, and I had to live with it.

Emil and I were great friends to begin with. We moved in the same circle for years, but she and I turned out to be closer than anyone in the group. In spite of how long I knew her. I couldn't give her a pass on this situation. Sometimes you gotta know when to just cut your losses with people and keep it moving. Some folks and some things you gotta just charge to the game, and keep the change.

<u>*You, Me, and He*</u>

It took about a year before I spoke to Emil again,
but I still hadn't forgiven her two-faced self because
she took it to a whole other level. She had moved
into a house with Bailey. Boy, was I in left field
when I said he was gay!

Late one night I got a phone call from Emil. She was
boo-hoo crying, saying that she couldn't believe
Bailey hadn't come home and it was almost 3
o'clock in the morning. "I know he's cheating; I can
feel it. Please go with me to look for him."

What the what? I hadn't spoken to this chick in a
year, but she wanted me to ride shotgun to go see

about a man I used to see that she was now seeing

to see if he was seeing someone else. I laughed and

said, "You want me to do what? Oh no, honey, I'm

in the bed." However, the nosy side got the best of

me so I asked, "And why do you think he's

cheating?"

"He's been taking or making phone calls in private,

suddenly spending tons of time at work, he started

to dress a little differently, he picks fights then

leaves the house, he doesn't touch me as much, and

on top of that, I think he changed his cologne."

Well, she had all the major signs of infidelity. As

much as I felt bad for her, there was no way in hell I

was getting out of my bed for that nonsense, and

plus she was on the "I ain't fucking with you no

more" list, and I gladly let her know that.

She sadly said, "Wow, so you're going to do me like that?"

"Did you expect me to say 'yeah, girl, I will be there in five minutes, we about to go find out what he doing'?"

"Well, yeah. We've known each other for almost twenty-two years," she said.

I started laughing hysterically. "Chile, please, you lost that privilege when you decided to date my ex!"

I guess that night I opened the floodgates since I stayed on the phone to talk with her, because all of sudden she started calling like we were friends again to discuss her relationship problems. Don't judge me. I was a softy sometimes. Don't get me wrong we didn't start hanging out or anything, but she needed my "expertise" on how to bust him. I don't know what she was calling me for though because she wasn't with all the brilliant ideas I came up with. I told her to go stake out his job and see what was going on or look in his call log, e-mails, and texts. She said she didn't want to snoop. I told her, "Don't think of it as snooping; think of it as checking. You know, like checking to see if he acting right." She still didn't want to follow my lead, so I didn't know what else to tell her.

Emil had to go on a trip to do make-up on a set of a movie. She was skeptical about going since she and Bailey were having problems. Emil's trip didn't last as long as she thought. She ended up leaving two days ahead of time. She attempted a few times that morning to let Bailey know she would be returning soon, but her calls went unanswered. She attempted one last time to call, but still got no answer. She even tried sending a couple of texts saying "hey". Since there was no response, she didn't bother to let know him she was boarding a flight to come home. She caught the Super Shuttle home.

As it pulled up to her house, she noticed that it seemed a little dark even though Bailey's car was in the driveway. As she opened the door, she set her suitcase down and took off her heels. She unbuttoned her blazer and placed it on the coat rack. She started to move towards the kitchen and she smelled the aroma of spaghetti. When she entered the kitchen, she saw some plates and glasses by the sink. As she walked in the dining room, she saw the table had candles that had been burned.

She turned to go back towards the front door, but hooked a left to go up the stairway. As she hit the top of the stairs, she turned to her right to see that the double doors to her bedroom were closed. She tiptoed to the bedroom and she placed her ear against the door. She reached down and gently turned the knob. As the door opened she peeked her head in and saw more candles and the bed in shambles, and sex was in the air.

As she stepped further into the room, she noticed champagne glasses, an empty bottle of Moët, and a bowl of strawberries on the night stand. As her eyes searched the room, she saw pieces of clothing scattered over the floor. She began to walk towards the bathroom, where she heard some sexy jazz music playing. She could hear the shower running.

She heard the giggle of a woman as she approached. Her heart began to pound as she finally entered from the hallway in the bathroom.

"Baby, I'm home," Emil announced.

She was startled to find Bailey standing in the shower kissing another woman while rubbing and rinsing the hairy chest of a man. Emil stood there in shock as Bailey said nonchalantly, "Hey babe, this Spencer. Spencer, this is Emil."

Spencer said, "Hey there" as he stood in the shower.

"Oh, and Emil, this is Lisa. Lisa, this is Emil."

Emil said, "Oh my God, this can't be happening right now! This is unreal!" She began to walk out of the bathroom while holding the wall for support.

She sat on the side of the bed, repeating over and over again, "This just can't be happening!" She began to beat her head with her fist in frustration. She heard the light switch click. She looked up it was Spencer turning on the light to gather his and Lisa's clothes.

He said, "We're just going to see our way out."

She sat there with tears in her eyes as she watched them exit from the bedroom. "Who are they, Bailey?" she yelled.

"I met them at a private swinger's club I host every week." Bailey came in and sat next to her and placed his arm around her shoulder. He whispered in her ear, "You okay?"

"What a silly question to ask! Of course I'm not okay. What is wrong with you?"

"What do you mean what is wrong with me?"

"Bailey, were you not just standing there lathering up a grown man? And you ask me what's wrong with me? Get your hands off of me! She began to get up. "You're crazy! You're out of your mind! You are sick to think I'd be okay with it. Wait, did you just say you host a swinger's club?"

Bailey fired back, "What's your problem, babe? I thought you were okay with this. After all, didn't Kennedee tell you I was gay?"

"Huh, yes, but I thought she was just lying and being jealous of what we have!" exclaimed Emil.

"Never once did I deny her accusations, did I? I'm not openly gay; I like men, but I like women as well. What's wrong with that?"

Emil yelled, "You just put my life in jeopardy! I could have contracted HIV because I trusted you, and what do you do? You turn around and betray me. I was quick to jump into the sack with you and committed to being in this relationship with integrity."

He said, "It's about us talking to each other about our sexual partners without worrying about being judged. It's my alternative sexuality. Hell, I organize the largest swinging events in LA. I am a gay man who occasionally enjoys women. I enjoy being a swinger. Either you're going to deal with it or you can leave. So what ya gonna do?"

When she told me what went down, I wasn't surprised. This was an awkward situation right here, but still hilarious and by far a "what the fuck" moment. Hell, I'm not surprised either, cuz anyone could have seen that from a mile away. So I asked her what happened next.

She said, "We're going to have an open relationship."

I yelled, "Hell to the naw! What the hell is an open relationship?"

"Kennedee, you wouldn't understand. We're like kindred spirits. He is the man of my dreams, and I could not face the rest of my life without the man of my dreams. I'd be miserable and guilt-ridden for leaving him over being a swinger or gay or whatever he is."

I just felt like going over there and slapping some sense into her. She was thirty-five she still had plenty of time to find someone else if she chose. She just didn't have to stay with Bailey. This relationship wasn't just harmful; it was also life-threatening. It was never that serious to compromise your standards and integrity just to say you have a man. Well, at least it never was for me.

I didn't know if I was more displeased that she was still staying with him or that her disloyal ass had hooked up with him in the first place. All I know is I knew I was right about him being gay, bisexual, whatever, and I was so happy I wasn't in this predicament. Never once did I say "I told you so". There was no need to gloat about my instincts being dead on. It was her decision, but I still found myself feeling morally icky. The full emotional effect of the betrayal had long sunk in when she decided to be with my ex.

I just said, "Look, girl, do whatever you like. Be straight, be gay, be a swinger, or a freak, whatever you like. I just know one thing. I ain't mad at you, but I ain't fucking with you no more."

I heard her gasp as I was putting the phone receiver down. I might have been right about Bailey's sexual preference, and I probably could have gotten past this whole situation. It was one thing to be a stank hoe with Sage's brother and cousin, but there's nothing quite like a "friend" who betrays you over some dick. You can't ever be my friend trying to compete with me, being low-key jealous of me and going after what's mine. If I couldn't trust you to be around my ex, I damn sure couldn't trust you with my current. Man, there were rules to this shit. She had broken quite a few. I was done with her. Once you do me shady, that's who you will always be to me.

14

A Friend Like Me

So that's what had happened. Do not confuse these ladies with my ride-or-die from my other book. They wasn't built to be ride-or-die chicks. These ladies actually were the ones that attempted to talk me out of my shenanigans, but had no reservations about trying to include me or asking me for help in their crazy situations. I eventually learned that I had rollers and not riders on my team. And trust me, there is a big difference between the two.

Sorry there was no get-back, payback, or getting even. I'ma just keep it moving. I told y'all to leave the petty shit to the petty bitches. I'ma just check you once on it, and after that be done with it. No

need to keep going back and forth with all that rah-
rah stuff with folks I thought was my friends. If it
fell through the cracks in my last book, let me make
it clear: my actions were petty even then with the
men. I don't want anyone to ever think that I was
glorifying my past. Although it was quite an
adventure getting even with those men, all I wanted
to do was share what happened in my life so
someone could do better than me in their
relationships, or for someone to know that they're
not the only one who have experienced some kinda
crazy drama in their life.

Just like in this story. Some of us have experienced
some type of drama in our friendships. However,
unlike the friendships that are depicted on reality
TV, the drama is not for ratings or a cast thrown

together that is now all of a sudden "friends". We decide who we allow to come in or stay in our circle. In spite of all the differences, we never once threw drinks, turned over tables, or hurled a bottle across the room. Not that I didn't think about it. But grown women don't handle situations like that. There was no reason to demean myself to make it on World Star, because that's not how I operate when it came to my friends. I made a few idle threats to scare a few of them. But at the end of the day I truly held my friendships to heart because they were like my family. Ultimately, how you handle the situation is what really counts. I don't want credit for being honest, loyal, and dependable. I will be the first person to admit that I have too many flaws to be perfect. But I'm a solid chick.

There is nothing worse to me than half-ass loyalty. Being loyal is the standard, not an option for me.

These were not the same young women I grew to love as a child. I don't know who the hell these chicks were. Some say that people don't change, they just reveal who they are. I beg to differ. I agree with the part that people don't change, but people do reveal who they are early on. Sometimes we just continue to roll with them knowing what they bring to the table. Snakes, rats, traitors, and backstabbers are not that easy to identify because at some point they had to be on your side. I would be lying if I said I was clueless of these women's characteristics because in the beginning of the story, I shared their characteristics. They showed me who they were from the beginning. The only difference as we got older was that the behavior only intensified and was no longer acceptable.

At some point in our lives, we've all had a friend part from the circle. We've all had to weigh friends' good and bad traits to truly see if it was worth the friendship, then determined that the drama wasn't worth it anymore and backed away from the situation. Not all friendships last forever. Social media should be thanked for keeping many friendships on life support these days. But if the friendship has simply run its course, don't be afraid to snatch that lifeline and let the friendship die.

Friends can be toxic and suck you dry in every aspect of your life if they're given enough opportunity. I've learned that how people treat you is their karma, and how you respond is yours.

Knowing when to move on from the drama is the first step.

As I grew older, I had a good sense of what kind of friends I wanted to have in my space, because with friends like these I didn't need enemies. When you grow, mature, and start experiencing more of life, your opinions change, your definition of real evolves. Some people got two different sets of rules: the ones they expect everybody else to live by, and the ones they live by. I never wanted or expected something from my circle that I wasn't willing to give. I just wanted folks to match my effort, always be honest, and stay consistent.

Folks walk around saying "no new friends". Don't be fooled by the hype. No one ever knows what their life may bring or who it may bring. But just know that it may be for a season, reason, or lifetime. Despite it all, I am still continuing to cultivate new friendships, associates, and acquaintances. Space is valuable and limited 'round me, so we gotta be adding value to each other. I don't have no problem cuttin' off dead weight, and negative folks. I have no room for 'em. Remember, you're only as good as the people you surround yourself with. Don't let loyalty become slavery. Be brave enough to let go of the ones that no longer offer any value to the friendship.

You can either learn from your pain or be destroyed by it. Everything depends on where your thoughts are. You control what you think about and you will control your life. When I think about Chloe, Sage, Talia, and Emil, I find myself pulling out my scrapbooks to reminisce about the good times that we shared at the beach, jazz festivals, spa, bowling, cruising on Crenshaw, and our old-school Polaroid shots at the clubs. I always thought because I started off with these folks, I would last 'til the end of time with them. With all these memories that we had, I look at them and I wonder what happened to the friendships we once had. I would be lying if I said I didn't miss them because they hold pieces of my childhood, and adulthood history.

Don't misconstrue the story. I'm not mad at any of these ladies. I'm more disappointed with them than anything. I just expected better from them. Would I ever sit down and have a drink to talk over something? Honestly, probably not due to drama, man issues, cattiness, or anything else that made me question their trust, loyalty, or integrity. I reward loyalty with love, and doubt with distance. I never allowed anyone to harden my heart; I just learned from the lessons. Being a leader sometimes requires you to stand alone, and I'm okay with that.

I'm a builder, not a destroyer. I'ma add, lift up, and encourage in every situation I step to...or I'ma just keep it moving. I salute the women who have remained loyal to their friendships over the years, because not everyone is able to do that. Loyalty is rare. If you find it, keep it. But for the ladies that can understand where I'm coming from, cheers to getting rid of friends like these.

About the Author

Kennedee Devoe is the author of Amazon Bestseller *Two Wrongs Don't Make a Right...It Makes Us Even.* She is CEO and Publisher of Devoe Publications. She also works in the nonprofit sector as a Program Director, and she has an Associate's degree in Early Childhood Studies, a Bachelor's degree in Business Management, and a Master's degree in Human Services. She hails from Carson, CA, and currently resides in the Los Angeles area.

Kennedee's Contact Information:

www.kdevoe.com

kennedeedevoe@yahoo.com

www.facebook.com/kennedeedevoe

www.twitter.com/kennedeedevoe

Instagram: @itmustbekd

www.youtube.com/kennedeedevoe

Book Kennedee for an appearance at your next book club meeting, relationship event, or women's group.

Did you enjoy the book? Feed an author.

Spread the word...not the book.

Please recommend to family and friends

Available on Amazon, Kindle, Nook, Barnes and Noble, and local bookstores.

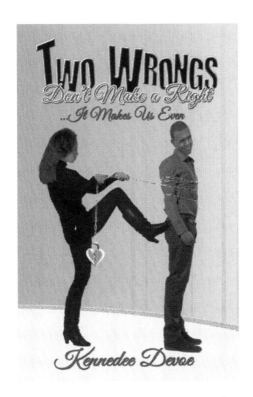

Check out Kennedee's first book

New release from Kennedee
coming summer 2015.

Stay tuned!

Check out our services at
www.kdevoe.com

30380837R00141

Made in the USA
Charleston, SC
13 June 2014